AF333355

Public Office Index
Volume 1

For my parents,
Everett and Frances,
who are, quite simply,
the very best.

Public Office Index

Volume 1

*U.S. Presidents, Vice Presidents,
Cabinet Members,
Supreme Court Justices*

Compiled by
Keith L. Justice

McFarland & Company, Inc., Publishers
Jefferson, North Carolina, and London

Library of Congress Cataloging in Publication Data

Justice, Keith L.
  Public office index.

  Includes index.
  Contents: v. 1. U.S. presidents, vice presidents,
cabinet members, supreme court justices.
  1. United States—Officials and employees—History—
Directories. 2. United States—Politics and government
—Directories. I. Title.
JK7 1985   353.002   84-43216

ISBN 0-89950-137-0 (alk. paper)

Printed in the United States of America

McFarland   Box 611   Jefferson NC 28640

Preface

The *Public Office Index* came about almost by accident. About three years ago I wondered—and the reason why I would wonder such a thing has long since escaped me—at what time in our history were the greatest number of retired presidents living at the same time. I devised a simple "time line" computer project to find out, unaware that the answer to my question was to be found in Joseph W. Kane's book, *Facts About the Presidents*.

Eventually I figured out the answer on my own. But somewhere along the way I realized it might be interesting to find out the same thing about other public offices, such as the vice presidency or the presidential cabinet. It was while researching the birth and death dates of the people who served in major public offices that I realized I was being forced to use the research facilities of several libraries just to find out a few simple dates.

It became clear that the most basic information about major officeholders should be available in a single-volume format. After all—my reasoning went—the vast majority of all inquiries into most public offices and officeholders could be answered by a book providing an index of administrations showing what cabinet members and vice presidents served what presidents, lists of succession for each office, biographical lists with dates of appointment or inauguration, birth and death, and other pertinent dates (depending on the office), plus a combination index and cross reference.

Because such a book apparently did not exist, it seemed a fine idea to compile one. It is hoped that this completed index will provide researchers, students, and others with a simple and easy way to find out facts—such as dates of appointment or confirmation—that are often slighted or ignored in other reference volumes. Even important biographical essays in landmark reference works often leave out exact dates, and while it might be nice to know that a certain cabinet member served 1804–1806, in some cases it might be much more helpful to know he was appointed on March 10, 1804, confirmed on March 15, 1804, and served until October 28, 1806.

If this index makes research on public offices and officeholders a little easier for anyone who must undertake such research, then it was well worth the effort.

Acknowledgments

No book is ever written or compiled in a vacuum. Throughout every step of the process there are many people who have an impact on the shape or direction of the project. For help — either direct or indirect — in completing this book I would like to extend special thanks to the staffs of the Union Public Library, Union, Mississippi; the Marion Public Library, Marion, Ohio; and the Mitchell Memorial Library, Mississippi State University, Starkville, Mississippi.

I would like also to express my thanks to Mary Majure and Daree Breland, whose kindness and generosity allowed the completion of this book, and to my wife, Virginia, who not only put up with me and the book for many months, but who also served above and beyond the call of duty by helping to research many of the dates recorded herein.

Needless to say, any imperfections or mistakes in the book have occurred in spite of the generous help of others, and all such mistakes are entirely my own responsibility.

Table of Contents

Introduction

The lists and indexes in this volume are mostly self-explanatory. The Administration Index provides a list of the elected vice presidents and appointed cabinet members who served each president; the succession lists show the order in which appointees or electees filled a given post; the biographical sections give very basic biographical information about each officeholder; and the name index acts as a cross reference to tell the researcher not only who is represented in the book, but how many different offices were held at one time or another by each officeholder.

Of more immediate concern to the researcher is the accuracy of the dates presented here. The answer to that question lies in an explanation of the methods used to determine some of the dates.

Presidential inaugurations occur on certain days, and these days—which normally occur about every four years—are extremely well documented. The span of a president's administration, and even the day of his inauguration, are fixed by law. Finding out the starting and ending dates of each president's administration was perhaps the simplest part of compiling this index. The appointment, confirmation, and resignation dates for Supreme Court justices are also well documented.

But the presidents' cabinets, and the men and women who have served in them, are an entirely different matter. Exact dates for the assumption and resignation of cabinet offices can be extremely difficult to find. There are, in fact, a number of different dates which could be valid areas of inquiry for each office. There is the day upon which the cabinet member was appointed; the day he or she was confirmed; the day he or she took the oath of office; and, in some cases, the first "official" day in office. Then there is the matter of the day a resignation is tendered or requested; the day it becomes effective; and the day the incumbent actually spends as the "last" day in office.

It would have been beyond the scope of this index to locate and present all of these dates for each office. Aside from the many years of research and the vast amount of travel required to unearth the information, there is the question of whether the dates would be of sufficient value to the prospective user of this index to warrant inclusion.

The decision was made to limit the dates to those which seemed to be of the greatest general interest and utility. When a cabinet post was vacated and reassigned during the course of an administration, it was assumed that the previous cabinet member held the post officially until the new appointee could be confirmed. In a few isolated cases the cabinet official served an extended period of time before confirmation, and in at least one case there was never any confirmation at all, so for these officials the date of entering office is the same as the date of appointment.

Time spent in office was calculated from the day of confirmation; and if the date of confirmation could not be identified but the date of swearing-in for the office could, then the tenure in office was calculated from that date. When either a date of appointment or a date of confirmation could be discovered, but not both, the same date was used to fill both blanks in the biographical entry.

The totals given for years, months, and days in office (or time spent in retirement, or time elapsed from retirement from an office until death even if other offices were held in the interim) are intended to be close approximations for general guidance and comparison only. These totals were computed in this fashion; If an officeholder was confirmed on March 28, 1885 and resigned effective September 29, 1891, his time in office would be figured as six years (1891 to 1885), six months (March 28 to September 28), and one day (28–29). The total will be given in the index as "6y 6m 1d." When days had to be counted (for example, March 2 to April 1 = 30 days), the answer was given as one month. Any number of days less than 30 was rendered simply as that number of days.

In some few cases (as for instance with Benjamin Stoddert) the exact date of birth was unknown. The year of birth was discoverable for every officeholder in this index, so when the day and month of birth was unavailable, the officeholder's age at appointment, confirmation, resignation, birth, and death were figured as if the officeholder had been born on the last day of his birth year. For this reason, the ages given for those whose exact day and month of birth were not known are accurate only to plus or minus one year.

Abbreviations

Because the number of offices represented here is actually rather small, but the number of people who have held the offices quite large, the avoidance of constant repetition of long office titles such as "Secretary of State" or "Secretary of the Treasury" required the development of a series of two-letter codes for each office. The coding system is quite simple, and in fact, the reader could probably guess correctly more than half of the coded office designations without looking at the list. There is no single code for the Supreme Court; instead, the justices are coded as AJ or CJ for Associate Justice or Chief Justice, whichever is appropriate (or in some few cases, both).

AG	Secretary of Agriculture
AT	Attorney General
AJ	Associate Justice
CJ	Chief Justice
CL	Secretary of Commerce and Labor
CM	Secretary of Commerce
DF	Secretary of Defense
ED	Secretary of Education
EN	Secretary of Energy
HD	Secretary of Housing and Urban Development
HH	Secretary of Health and Human Services
HW	Secretary of Health, Education and Welfare
IN	Secretary of the Interior
LB	Secretary of Labor
NV	Secretary of the Navy
PG	Postmaster General
PR	President
ST	Secretary of State
TR	Secretary of Transportation
TY	Secretary of the Treasury
VP	Vice President
WR	Secretary of War

Administration Index

George Washington 1789-1797
Vice President
John Adams 1789-1797
Secretary of State
Thomas Jefferson 1789-1794
Edmund Randolph 1794-1795
Timothy Pickering 1795-1797
Secretary of the Treasury
Alexander Hamilton 1789-1795
Oliver Wolcott 1795-1797
Secretary of War
Henry Knox 1789-1795
Timothy Pickering 1795
James McHenry 1795-1797
Attorney General
Edmund Randolph 1789-1794
William Bradford 1794-1795
Charles Lee 1795-1797
Postmaster General
Samuel Osgood 1789-1791
Timothy Pickering 1791-1795
Joseph Habersham 1795-1797

John Adams 1797-1801
Vice President
Thomas Jefferson 1797-1801
Secretary of State
Timothy Pickering 1797-1800
John Marshall 1800-1801
Secretary of the Treasury
Oliver Wolcott 1797-1800
Samuel Dexter 1801

Secretary of War
James McHenry 1797-1800
Samuel Dexter 1800
Attorney General
Charles Lee 1797-1801
Postmaster General
Joseph Habersham 1797-1801
Secretary of the Navy
Benjamin Stoddert 1798-1801

Thomas Jefferson 1801-1809
Vice President
Aaron Burr 1801-1805
George Clinton 1805-1809
Secretary of State
James Madison 1801-1809
Secretary of the Treasury
Samuel Dexter 1801
Albert Gallatin 1801-1809
Secretary of War
Henry Dearborn 1801-1809
Attorney General
Levi Lincoln 1801-1804
John Breckenridge 1805-1806
Caesar A. Rodney 1807
Postmaster General
Joseph Habersham 1801
Gideon Granger 1801-1809
Secretary of the Navy
Benjamin Stoddert 1801
Robert Smith 1801-1809

James Madison 1809–1817
Vice President
George Clinton 1809–1812
Elbridge Gerry 1813–1817
Secretary of State
Robert Smith 1809–1811
James Monroe 1811–1814, 1815–1817
Secretary of the Treasury
Albert Gallatin 1809–1814
George W. Campbell 1814
Alexander J. Dallas 1814–1816
William H. Crawford 1816–1817
Secretary of War
William Eustis 1809–1812
John Armstrong 1813–1814
James Monroe 1814–1815
William H. Crawford 1815–1816
Attorney General
Caesar A. Rodney 1809–1811
William Pinkney 1811–1814
Richard Rush 1814–1817
Postmaster General
Gideon Granger 1809–1814
Return J. Meigs, Jr. 1814–1817
Secretary of the Navy
Paul Hamilton 1809–1812
William Jones 1813–1814
Benjamin W. Crowninshield
1814–1817

James Monroe 1817–1825
Vice President
Daniel D. Tompkins 1817–1825
Secretary of State
John Q. Adams 1817–1825
Secretary of the Treasury
William H. Crawford 1817–1825
Secretary of War
John C. Calhoun 1817–1825
Attorney General
Richard Rush 1817
William Wirt 1817–1825

Postmaster General
Return J. Meigs Jr. 1817–1823
John McLean 1823–1825
Secretary of the Navy
Benjamin W. Crowninshield
1817–1818
Smith Thompson 1818–1823
Samuel L. Southard 1823–1825

John Quincy Adams 1825–1829
Vice President
John C. Calhoun 1825–1829
Secretary of State
Henry Clay 1825–1829
Secretary of the Treasury
Richard Rush 1825–1829
Secretary of War
James Barbour 1825–1828
Peter B. Porter 1828–1829
Attorney General
William Wirt 1825–1829
Postmaster General
John McLean 1825–1829
Secretary of the Navy
Samuel L. Southard 1825–1829

Andrew Jackson 1829–1837
Vice President
John C. Calhoun 1829–1832
Martin Van Buren 1833–1837
Secretary of State
Martin Van Buren 1829–1831
Edward Livingston 1831–1833
Louis McLane 1833–1834
John Forsyth 1834–1837
Secretary of the Treasury
Samuel D. Ingham 1829–1831
Louis McLane 1831–1833
William J. Duane 1833
Roger B. Taney 1833–1834
Levi Woodbury 1834–1837

Secretary of War
  John H. Eaton 1829–1831
  Lewis Cass 1831–1836
Attorney General
  John M. Berrien 1829–1831
  Roger B. Taney 1831–1833
  Benjamin F. Butler 1833–1837
Postmaster General
  William T. Barry 1829–1835
  Amos Kendall 1835–1837
Secretary of the Navy
  John Branch 1829–1831
  Levi Woodbury 1831–1834
  Mahlon Dickerson 1834–1837

Martin Van Buren 1837–1841
Vice President
  Richard M. Johnson 1837–1841
Secretary of State
  John Forsyth 1837–1841
Secretary of the Treasury
  Levi Woodbury 1837–1841
Secretary of War
  Joel R. Poinsett 1837–1841
Attorney General
  Benjamin F. Butler 1837–1838
  Felix Grundy 1838–1840
  Henry Dilworth 1840–1841
Postmaster General
  Amos Kendall 1837–1840
  John M. Niles 1840–1841
Secretary of the Navy
  Mahlon Dickerson 1837–1838
  James K. Paulding 1838–1841

William Henry Harrison 1841
Vice President
  John Tyler 1841
Secretary of State
  Daniel Webster 1841
Secretary of the Treasury
  Thomas Ewing 1841

Secretary of War
  John Bell 1841
Attorney General
  John J. Crittenden 1841
Postmaster General
  Francis Granger 1841
Secretary of the Navy
  George E. Badger 1841

John Tyler 1841–1845
Secretary of State
  Daniel Webster 1841–1843
  Abel P. Upshur 1843–1844
  John C. Calhoun 1844–1845
Secretary of the Treasury
  Thomas Ewing 1841
  Walter Forward 1841–1843
  John C. Spencer 1843–1844
  George M. Bibb 1844–1845
Secretary of War
  John Bell 1841
  John C. Spencer 1841–1843
  James M. Porter 1843–1844
  William Wilkins 1844–1845
Attorney General
  John C. Crittenden 1841
  Hugh S. Legare 1841–1843
  John Nelson 1843–1845
Postmaster General
  Francis Granger 1841
  Charles A. Wickliffe 1841–1845
Secretary of the Navy
  George E. Badger 1841
  Abel P. Upshur 1841–1843
  David Henshaw 1843–1844
  Thomas W. Gilmer 1844
  John Y. Mason 1844–1845

James K. Polk 1845–1849
Vice President
  George M. Dallas 1845–1849

Secretary of State
James Buchanan 1845–1849
Secretary of the Treasury
Robert J. Walker 1845–1849
Secretary of War
William L. Marcy 1845–1849
Attorney General
John Y. Mason 1845–1846
Nathan Clifford 1846–1848
Isaac Toucey 1848–1849
Postmaster General
Cave Johnson 1845–1849
Secretary of the Navy
George Bancroft 1845–1846
John Y. Mason 1846–1849

Zachary Taylor 1849–1850
Vice President
Millard Fillmore 1849–1850
Secretary of State
John M. Clayton 1849–1850
Secretary of the Treasury
William A. Meredith 1849–1850
Secretary of War
George W. Crawford 1849–1850
Attorney General
Reverdy Johnson 1849–1850
Postmaster General
Jacob Collamer 1849–1850
Secretary of the Navy
William B. Preston 1849–1850
Secretary of the Interior
Thomas Ewing 1849–1850

Millard Fillmore 1850–1853
Secretary of State
Daniel Webster 1850–1852
Edward Everett 1852–1853
Secretary of the Treasury
Thomas Corwin 1850–1853
Secretary of War
Charles M. Conrad 1850–1853

Attorney General
John J. Crittenden 1850–1853
Postmaster General
Nathan K. Hall 1850–1852
Samuel D. Hubbard 1852–1853
Secretary of the Navy
William A. Graham 1850–1852
John P. Kennedy 1852–1853
Secretary of the Interior
Thomas M.T. McKennan 1850
Alexander H. Holmes 1850–1853

Franklin Pierce 1853–1857
Vice President
William R. King 1853
Secretary of State
William L. Marcy 1853–1857
Secretary of the Treasury
James Guthrie 1853–1857
Secretary of War
Jefferson Davis 1853–1857
Attorney General
Caleb Cushing 1853–1857
Postmaster General
James Campbell 1853–1857
Secretary of the Navy
James C. Dobbin 1853–1857
Secretary of the Interior
Robert McClelland 1853–1857

James Buchanan 1857–1861
Vice President
John C. Breckenridge 1857–1861
Secretary of State
Lewis Cass 1857–1860
Jeremiah S. Black 1860–1861
Secretary of the Treasury
Howell Cobb 1857–1860
Phillip F. Thomas 1860–1861
John A. Dix 1861
Secretary of War
John B. Floyd 1857–1861

Attorney General
Jeremiah S. Black 1857–1860
Edwin M. Stanton 1860–1861
Postmaster General
Aaron V. Brown 1857–1859
Joseph Holt 1859–1861
Horatio King 1861
Secretary of the Navy
Isaac Toucey 1857–1861
Secretary of the Interior
Jacob Thompson 1857–1861

Abraham Lincoln 1861–1865
Vice President
Hannibal Hamlin 1861–1865
Andrew Johnson 1865
Secretary of State
William H. Seward 1861–1865
Secretary of the Treasury
Salmon P. Chase 1861–1864
William P. Fessenden 1864–1865
Hugh McCulloch 1865
Secretary of War
Simon Cameron 1861–1862
Edwin M. Stanton 1862–1865
Attorney General
Edward Bates 1861–1864
James Speed 1864–1865
Postmaster General
Montgomery Blair 1861–1864
William Dennison 1864–1865
Secretary of the Navy
Gideon Welles 1861–1865
Secretary of the Interior
Caleb B. Smith 1861–1863
John P. Usher 1863–1865

Andrew Johnson 1865–1869
Secretary of State
William H. Seward 1865–1869
Secretary of the Treasury
Hugh McCulloch 1865–1869

Secretary of War
Edwin M. Stanton 1865–1867
Edwin M. Stanton 1868
John M. Schofield 1868–1869
Attorney General
James Speed 1865–1866
Henry Stanbery 1866–1868
William A. Evarts 1868–1869
Postmaster General
William Dennison 1865–1866
Alexander W. Randall 1866–1869
Secretary of the Navy
Gideon Welles 1865–1869
Secretary of the Interior
John P. Usher 1865
James Harlan 1865–1866
Orville H. Browning 1866–1869

Ulysses S. Grant 1869–1877

Vice President
Schuyler Colfax 1869–1873
Henry Wilson 1873–1877
Secretary of State
Elihu B. Washburne 1869
Hamilton Fish 1869–1877
Secretary of the Treasury
George S. Boutwell 1869–1873
William A. Richardson 1873–1874
Benjamin H. Bristow 1874–1876
Lot M. Morrill 1876–1877
Secretary of War
John A. Rawlins 1869
William T. Sherman 1869
William W. Belknap 1869–1876
Alphonso Taft 1876
James D. Cameron 1876–1877
Attorney General
Ebenezer R. Hoar 1869–1870
Amos T. Akerman 1870–1872
George H. Williams 1872–1875
Edward Pierrepont 1875–1876
Alphonso Taft 1876–1877

Postmaster General
  John A.J. Creswell 1869–1874
  James W. Marshall 1874
  Marshall Jewell 1874–1876
  James N. Tyner 1876–1877
Secretary of the Navy
  Adolph E. Borie 1869
  George M. Robeson 1869–1877
Secretary of the Interior
  Jacob D. Cox 1869–1870
  Columbus O. Delano 1870–1875
  Zachariah Chandler 1875–1877

Rutherford B. Hayes 1877–1881
Vice President
  William A. Wheeler 1877–1881
Secretary of State
  William A. Evarts 1877–1881
Secretary of the Treasury
  John Sherman 1877–1881
Secretary of War
  George W. McCrary 1877–1879
  Alexander Ramsey 1879–1881
Attorney General
  Charles Devens 1877–1881
Postmaster General
  David M. Key 1877–1880
  Horace Maynard 1880–1881
Secretary of the Navy
  Richard W. Thompson 1877–1880
  Nathan Goff, Jr. 1881
Secretary of the Interior
  Carl Schurz 1877–1881

James A. Garfield 1881
Vice President
  Chester A. Arthur 1881
Secretary of State
  James G. Blaine 1881
Secretary of the Treasury
  William Windom 1881

Secretary of War
  Robert T. Lincoln 1881
Attorney General
  Wayne McVeagh 1881
Postmaster General
  Thomas L. James 1881
Secretary of the Navy
  William H. Hunt 1881
Secretary of the Interior
  Samuel J. Kirkwood 1881

Chester A. Arthur 1881–1885
Secretary of State
  James G. Blaine 1881
  Frederick T. Frelinghuysen 1881–
  1885
Secretary of the Treasury
  William Windom 1881
  Charles J. Folger 1881–1884
  Walter Q. Gresham 1884
  Hugh McCulloch 1884–1885
Secretary of War
  Robert T. Lincoln 1881–1885
Attorney General
  Wayne McVeagh 1881
  Benjamin H. Brewster 1881–1885
Postmaster General
  Thomas L. James 1881
  Timothy O. Howe 1882–1883
  Walter Q. Gresham 1883–1884
  Frank Hatton 1884–1885
Secretary of the Navy
  William H. Hunt 1881–1882
  William E. Chandler 1882–1885
Secretary of the Interior
  Samuel J. Kirkwood 1881–1882
  Henry M. Teller 1882–1885

Grover Cleveland 1885–1889
Vice President
  Thomas A. Hendricks 1885–1889

Secretary of State
Thomas F. Bayard 1885-1889
Secretary of the Treasury
Daniel Manning 1885-1887
Charles S. Fairchild 1887-1889
Secretary of War
William C. Endicott 1885-1889
Attorney General
Augustus H. Garland 1885-1889
Postmaster General
William F. Vilas 1885-1888
Donald M. Dickinson 1888-1889
Secretary of the Navy
William C. Whitney 1885-1889
Secretary of the Interior
Lucius Q.C. Lamar 1885-1888
William F. Vilas 1888-1889
Secretary of Agriculture
Norman J. Colman 1889

Benjamin Harrison 1889-1893
Vice President
Levi P. Morton 1889-1893
Secretary of State
James G. Blaine 1889-1892
John W. Foster 1892-1893
Secretary of the Treasury
William Windom 1889-1891
Charles Foster 1891-1893
Secretary of War
Redfield Proctor 1889-1891
Stephen B. Elkins 1891-1893
Attorney General
William H.H. Miller 1889-1893
Postmaster General
John Wanamaker 1889-1893
Secretary of the Navy
Benjamin F. Tracy 1889-1893
Secretary of the Interior
John W. Noble 1889-1893
Secretary of Agriculture
Jeremiah M. Rusk 1889-1893

Grover Cleveland 1893-1897
Vice President
Adlai E. Stevenson 1893-1897
Secretary of State
Walter Q. Gresham 1893-1895
Richard Olney 1895-1897
Secretary of the Treasury
John G. Carlisle 1893-1897
Secretary of War
Daniel S. Lamont 1893-1897
Attorney General
Richard Olney 1893-1895
Judson Harmon 1895-1897
Postmaster General
Wilson S. Bissell 1893-1895
William L. Wilson 1895-1897
Secretary of the Navy
Hilary A. Herbert 1893-1897
Secretary of the Interior
Hoke Smith 1893-1896
David R. Francis 1896-1897
Secretary of Agriculture
Julius S. Morton 1893-1897

William McKinley 1897-1901
Vice President
Garret A. Hobart 1897-1899
Theodore Roosevelt 1901
Secretary of State
John Sherman 1897-1898
William R. Day 1898
John Hay 1898-1901
Secretary of the Treasury
Lyman J. Gage 1897-1901
Secretary of War
Russell A. Alger 1897-1899
Elihu Root 1899-1901
Attorney General
Joseph McKenna 1897-1898
John W. Griggs 1898-1901
Philander C. Knox 1901
Postmaster General
James A. Gary 1897-1898
Charles E. Smith 1898-1901

Secretary of the Navy
John D. Long 1897–1901
Secretary of the Interior
Cornelius N. Bliss 1897–1899
Ethan A. Hitchcock 1899–1901
Secretary of Agriculture
James Wilson 1897–1901

Theodore Roosevelt 1901–1909
Vice President
Charles W. Fairbanks 1905–1909
Secretary of State
John Hay 1901–1905
Elihu Root 1905–1909
Robert Bacon 1909
Secretary of the Treasury
Lyman J. Gage 1901–1902
Leslie M. Shaw 1902–1907
George B. Cortelyou 1907–1909
Secretary of War
Elihu Root 1901–1904
William H. Taft 1904–1908
Luke E. Wright 1908–1909
Attorney General
Philander C. Knox 1901–1904
William H. Moody 1904–1906
Charles J. Bonaparte 1906–1909
Postmaster General
Charles E. Smith 1901–1902
Henry C. Payne 1902–1904
Robert J. Wynne 1904–1905
George B. Cortelyou 1905–1907
George Meyer 1907–1909
Secretary of the Navy
John D. Long 1901–1902
William H. Moody 1902–1904
Paul Morton 1904–1905
Charles J. Bonaparte 1905–1906
Victor H. Metcalf 1906–1908
Truman H. Newberry 1908–1909
Secretary of the Interior
Ethan A. Hitchcock 1901–1907
James R. Garfield 1907–1909

Secretary of Agriculture
James Wilson 1901–1909
Secretary of Commerce and Labor
George B. Cortelyou 1903–1904
Victor H. Metcalf 1904–1906
Oscar S. Straus 1906–1909

William H. Taft 1909–1913
Vice President
James S. Sherman 1909–1912
Secretary of State
Philander C. Knox 1909–1913
Secretary of the Treasury
Franklin MacVeagh 1909–1913
Secretary of War
Jacob M. Dickinson 1909–1911
Henry L. Stimson 1911–1913
Attorney General
George W. Wickersham 1909–1913
Postmaster General
Frank H. Hitchcock 1909–1913
Secretary of the Navy
George Meyer 1909–1913
Secretary of the Interior
Richard A. Ballinger 1909–1911
Walter W. Fisher 1911–1913
Secretary of Agriculture
James Wilson 1909–1913
Secretary of Commerce and Labor
Charles Nagel 1909–1913

Woodrow Wilson 1913–1921
Vice President
Thomas R. Marshall 1913–1921
Secretary of State
William J. Bryan 1913–1915
Robert Lansing 1915–1920
Bainbridge Colby 1920–1921
Secretary of the Treasury
William G. McAdoo 1913–1918
Carter Glass 1918–1920

David F. Houston 1920–1921
Secretary of War
Lindley M. Garrison 1913–1916
Newton D. Baker 1916–1921
Attorney General
James C. McReynolds 1913–1914
Thomas W. Gregory 1914–1919
Alexander M. Palmer 1919–1921
Postmaster General
Albert S. Burleson 1913–1921
Secretary of the Navy
Josephus Daniels 1913–1921
Secretary of the Interior
Franklin K. Lane 1913–1920
John B. Payne 1920–1921
Secretary of Agriculture
David F. Houston 1913–1920
Edwin T. Meredith 1919–1921
Secretary of Commerce
William C. Redfield 1913–1919
Joshua W. Alexander 1919–1920
Secretary of Labor
William B. Wilson 1913–1921

Warren G. Harding 1921–1923
Vice President
Calvin Coolidge 1921–1923
Secretary of State
Charles E. Hughes 1921–1923
Secretary of the Treasury
Andrew W. Mellon 1921–1923
Secretary of War
John W. Weeks 1921–1923
Attorney General
Harry M. Daugherty 1921–1923
Postmaster General
William H. Hays 1921–1922
Hubert Work 1922–1923
Harry S. New 1923
Secretary of the Navy
Edwin Denby 1921–1923
Secretary of the Interior
Albert B. Fall 1921–1923
Hubert Work 1923

Secretary of Agriculture
Henry C. Wallace 1921–1923
Secretary of Commerce
Herbert C. Hoover 1921–1923
Secretary of Labor
James J. Davis 1921–1923

Calvin Coolidge 1923–1929
Vice President
Charles G. Dawes 1925–1929
Secretary of State
Charles E. Hughes 1923–1925
Frank B. Kellogg 1925–1929
Secretary of the Treasury
Andrew W. Mellon 1923–1929
Secretary of War
John W. Weeks 1923–1925
Dwight F. Davis 1925–1929
Attorney General
Harry M. Daugherty 1923–1924
Harlan F. Stone 1924–1925
John G. Sargent 1925–1929
Postmaster General
Harry S. New 1923–1929
Secretary of the Navy
Edwin Denby 1923–1924
Curtis D. Wilbur 1924–1929
Secretary of the Interior
Hubert Work 1923–1928
Roy O. West 1929
Secretary of Agriculture
Henry C. Wallace 1923–1924
Howard M. Gore 1924–1925
William M. Jardine 1925–1929
Secretary of Commerce
Herbert Hoover 1923–1928
William F. Whiting 1928–1929
Secretary of Labor
James J. Davis 1923–1929

Herbert Hoover 1929-1933
Vice President
　Charles Curtis 1929-1933
Secretary of State
　Henry L. Stimson 1929-1933
Secretary of the Treasury
　Andrew W. Mellon 1929-1932
　Ogden L. Mills 1932-1933
Secretary of War
　James W. Good 1929
　Patrick J. Hurley 1929-1933
Attorney General
　William D. Mitchell 1929-1933
Postmaster General
　Walter F. Brown 1929-1933
Secretary of the Navy
　Charles F. Adams 1929-1933
Secretary of the Interior
　Ray L. Wilbur 1929-1933
Secretary of Agriculture
　Arthur M. Hyde 1929-1933
Secretary of Commerce
　Robert P. Lamont 1929-1932
　Roy D. Chapin 1932-1933
Secretary of Labor
　James J. Davis 1929-1930
　William N. Doak 1930-1933

Franklin D. Roosevelt 1933-1945
Vice President
　John N. Garner 1933-1941
　Henry A. Wallace 1941-1945
　Harry S Truman 1945
Secretary of State
　Cordell Hull 1933-1944
　E.R. Stettinius, Jr. 1944-1945
Secretary of the Treasury
　William H. Woodin 1933-1934
　Henry Morgenthau, Jr., 1934-
　1945
Secretary of War
　George H. Dern 1933-1936
　Harry H. Woodring 1937-1940
　Henry L. Stimson 1940-1945

Attorney General
　Homer S. Cummings 1933-1939
　Frank Murphy 1939-1940
　Robert H. Jackson 1940-1941
　Francis Biddle 1941-1945
Postmaster General
　James A. Farley 1933-1940
　Frank C. Walker 1940-1945
Secretary of the Navy
　Claude A. Swanson 1933-1939
　Charles Edison 1940
　Frank Knox 1940-1944
　James V. Forrestal 1944-1945
Secretary of the Interior
　Harold L. Ickes 1933-1945
Secretary of Agriculture
　Henry A. Wallace 1933-1940
　Claude R. Wickard 1940-1945
Secretary of Commerce
　Daniel C. Roper 1933-1938
　Harry L. Hopkins 1939-1940
　Jesse H. Jones 1940-1945
　Henry A. Wallace 1945
Secretary of Labor
　Frances Perkins 1933-1945

Harry S Truman 1945-1953
Vice President
　Alben W. Barkley 1949-1953
Secretary of State
　E.R. Stettinius, Jr. 1945
　James F. Byrnes 1945-1947
　George C. Marshall 1947-1949
　Dean G. Acheson 1949-1953
Secretary of the Treasury
　Henry Morgenthau, Jr. 1945
　Fred M. Vinson 1945-1946
　John W. Snyder 1946-1953
Secretary of War
　Henry L. Stimson 1945
　Robert P. Patterson 1945-1947
　Kenneth C. Royall 1947
Secretary of Defense
　James V. Forrestal 1947-1949

Charles S. Thomas 1954–1957
Thomas S. Gates, Jr. 1957–1958
William B. Franke 1958–1961

John F. Kennedy 1961–1963
Vice President
Lyndon B. Johnson 1961–1963
Secretary of State
Dean Rusk 1961–1963
Secretary of the Treasury
C. Douglas Dillon 1961–1963
Secretary of Defense
Robert S. McNamara 1961–1963
Attorney General
Robert F. Kennedy 1961–1963
Postmaster General
J. Edward Day 1961–1963
John A. Gronouski 1963
Secretary of the Interior
Stewart L. Udall 1961–1963
Secretary of Agriculture
Orville L. Freeman 1961–1963
Secretary of Commerce
Luther H. Hodges 1961–1963
Secretary of Labor
Arthur J. Goldberg 1961–1962
W. Willard Wirtz 1962–1963
*Secretary of Health, Education and
    Welfare*
Abraham A. Ribicoff 1961–1962
Anthony J. Celebrezze 1962–1963
Non-Cabinet Appointments:
Secretary of the Air Force
Eugene M. Zuckert 1961–1963
Secretary of the Army
Elvis J. Stahr, Jr. 1961–1962
Cyrus R. Vance 1962–1963
Secretary of the Navy
John B. Connally, Jr. 1961
Fred Korth 1961–1963

Lyndon B. Johnson 1963–1969
Vice President
Hubert H. Humphrey 1965–1969
Secretary of State
Dean Rusk 1963–1969
Secretary of the Treasury
C. Douglas Dillon 1963–1965
Henry H. Fowler 1965–1969
Joseph W. Barr 1968–1969
Secretary of Defense
Robert S. McNamara 1963–1968
Clark M. Clifford 1968–1969
Attorney General
Robert F. Kennedy 1963–1965
Nicholas D. Katzenbach 1965–
    1967
William R. Clark 1967–1969
Postmaster General
John A. Gronouski 1963–1965
Lawrence F. O'Brien 1965–1968
W. Marvin Watson 1968–1969
Secretary of the Interior
Stewart L. Udall 1963–1969
Secretary of Agriculture
Orville L. Freeman 1963–1969
Secretary of Commerce
Luther H. Hodges 1963–1965
John T. Connor 1965–1967
Alexander B. Trowbridge 1967–
    1968
Cyrus R. Smith 1968–1969
Secretary of Labor
W. Willard Wirtz 1963–1969
*Secretary of Health, Education and
    Welfare*
Anthony J. Celebrezze 1963–1965
John W. Gardner 1965–1968
Wilbur J. Cohen 1968–1969
*Secretary of Housing and Urban
    Development*
Robert R. Weaver 1966–1969
Robert C. Wood 1969
Secretary of Transportation
Alan S. Boyd 1967–1969
Non-Cabinet Appointments:

Secretary of the Air Force
Eugene M. Zuckert 1963–1965
Harold Brown 1965–1969
Secretary of the Army
Cyrus R. Vance 1963–1964
Stephen Ailes 1964–1965
Stanley R. Resor 1965–1969
Secretary of the Navy
Paul H. Nitze 1963–1967
John T. McNaughton 1967
Paul R. Ignatius 1967–1969

Richard M. Nixon 1969–1974
Vice President
Spiro T. Agnew 1969–1973
Gerald R. Ford 1973–1974
Secretary of State
William P. Rogers 1969–1973
Henry A. Kissinger 1973–1974
Secretary of the Treasury
David M. Kennedy 1969–1971
John B. Connally 1971–1972
George P. Shultz 1972–1974
William E. Simon 1974
Secretary of Defense
Melvin R. Laird 1969–1973
Elliot L. Richardson 1973
James R. Schlesinger 1973–1974
Attorney General
John N. Mitchell 1969–1972
Richard G. Kleindienst 1972–1973
Elliot L. Richardson 1973–1974
William B. Saxbe 1974
Postmaster General
Winton M. Blount 1969–1970
Secretary of the Interior
Walter J. Hickel 1969–1971
Rogers C.B. Morton 1971–1974
Secretary of Agriculture
Clifford M. Hardin 1969–1971
Earl L. Butz 1971–1974
Secretary of Commerce
Maurice H. Stans 1969–1972
Peter G. Peterson 1972–1973
Frederick B. Dent 1973–1974

Secretary of Labor
George P. Shultz 1969–1970
James D. Hodgson 1970–1973
Peter J. Brennan 1973–1974
Secretary of Health, Education and Welfare
Robert H. Finch 1969–1970
Elliot L. Richardson 1970–1973
Caspar W. Weinberger 1973–1974
Secretary of Housing and Urban Development
George W. Romney 1969–1973
James T. Lynn 1973–1974
Secretary of Transportation
John A. Volpe 1969–1974
Claude S. Brinegar 1974
Non-Cabinet Appointments:
Secretary of the Air Force
Robert C. Seamans, Jr. 1969–1973
John L. McLucas 1973–1974
Secretary of the Army
Stanley A. Resor 1969–1971
Robert F. Froehlke 1971–1973
Howard H. Callaway 1973–1974
Secretary of the Navy
John H. Chafee 1969–1972
John W. Warner 1972–1974

Gerald R. Ford 1974–1977
Vice President
Nelson A. Rockefeller 1974–1977
Secretary of State
Henry A. Kissinger 1974–1977
Secretary of the Treasury
William E. Simon 1974–1977
Secretary of Defense
James R. Schlesinger 1974–1975
Donald R. Rumsfeld 1975–1977
Attorney General
William B. Saxbe 1974–1975
Edward H. Levi 1975–1977
Secretary of the Interior
Rogers C.B. Morton 1974–1975

Stanley K. Hathaway 1975
Thomas S. Kleppe 1975–1977
Secretary of Agriculture
Earl L. Butz 1974–1976
John A. Knebel 1976–1977
Secretary of Commerce
Frederick B. Dent 1974–1975
Rogers C.B. Morton 1975
Elliot L. Richardson 1975–1977
Secretary of Labor
Peter J. Brennan 1974–1975
John T. Dunlop 1975–1976
W.J. Usery, Jr. 1976–1977
Secretary of Health, Education and
Welfare
Caspar W. Weinberger 1974–1975
Forrest D. Mathews 1975–1977
Secretary of Housing and Urban
Development
James T. Lynn 1974–1975
Carla A. Hills 1975–1977
Secretary of Transportation
Claude S. Brinegar 1974–1975
William T. Coleman, Jr. 1975–
1977
Non-Cabinet Appointments:
Secretary of the Air Force
John L. McLucas 1974–1976
Thomas C. Reed 1976–1977
Secretary of the Army
Howard H. Callaway 1974–1975
Martin R. Hoffman 1975–1977
Secretary of the Navy
J. William Middendorf II 1974–
1977

Jimmy [James Earl] Carter 1977–
1981
Vice President
Walter F. Mondale 1977–1981
Secretary of State
Cyrus R. Vance 1977–1980
Edmund S. Muskie 1980–1981

Secretary of the Treasury
W. Michael Blumenthal 1977–
1979
G. William Miller 1979–1981
Secretary of Defense
Harold Brown 1977–1981
Attorney General
Griffin B. Bell 1977–1979
Benjamin R. Civiletti 1979–1981
Secretary of the Interior
Cecil D. Andrus 1977–1981
Secretary of Agriculture
Bob Bergland 1977–1981
Secretary of Commerce
Juanita M. Kreps 1977–1979
Philip M. Klutznik 1979–1981
Secretary of Labor
F. Ray Marshall 1977–1981
Secretary of Health, Education and
Welfare
Joseph A. Califano, Jr. 1977–1979
Patricia R. Harris 1979
Secretary of Health and Human Services
Patricia R. Harris 1979–1981
Secretary of Education
Shirley Hufstedler 1979–1981
Secretary of Housing and Urban
Development
Patricia R. Harris 1977–1979
Moon Landrieu 1979–1981
Secretary of Transportation
Brock Adams 1977–1979
Neil E. Goldschmidt 1979–1981
Secretary of Energy
James R. Schlesinger 1977–1979
Robert W. Duncan, Jr. 1979–1981
Non-Cabinet Appointments:
Secretary of the Air Force
John C. Stetson 1977–1979
Hans M. Mark 1979–1981
Secretary of the Army
Clifford L. Alexander, Jr. 1977–
1981
Secretary of the Navy
W. Graham Claytor, Jr. 1977–
1979

Edward Hidalgo 1979–1981

Ronald Reagan 1981–
Vice President
George F. Bush 1981–
Secretary of State
Alexander M. Haig, Jr. 1981–
1982
George P. Shultz 1982–
Secretary of the Treasury
Donald T. Regan 1981–1985
James A. Baker III 1985–
Secretary of Defense
Caspar W. Weinberger 1981–
Attorney General
William F. Smith 1981–1985
Edwin Meese 1985–
Secretary of the Interior
James G. Watt 1981–1983
William P. Clark 1983–1985
Donald P. Hodel 1985–
Secretary of Agriculture
John R. Block 1981–
Secretary of Commerce
Malcolm Baldrige 1981–

Secretary of Labor
Raymond J. Donovan 1981–
Secretary of Health and Human Services
Richard S. Schweiker 1981–1983
Margaret M. Heckler 1983–
Secretary of Education
Terrel Bell 1981–1985
William J. Bennett 1985–
*Secretary of Housing and Urban
Development*
Samuel R. Pierce, Jr. 1981–
Secretary of Transportation
Andrew L. Lewis, Jr. 1981–1982
Elizabeth H. Dole 1982–
Secretary of Energy
James B. Edwards 1981–1982
Donald P. Hodel 1982–1985
John S. Herrington 1985–
Non-Cabinet Appointments:
Secretary of the Air Force
Verne Orr 1981–
Secretary of the Army
John O. Marsh, Jr. 1981–
Secretary of the Navy
John F. Lehman, Jr. 1981–

Presidential Succession

George Washington 1789–1797
John Adams 1797–1801
Thomas Jefferson 1801–1809
James Madison 1809–1817
James Monroe 1817–1825
John Quincy Adams 1825–1829
Andrew Jackson 1829–1837
Martin Van Buren 1837–1841
William Henry Harrison 1841
John Tyler 1841–1845
James K. Polk 1845–1849
Zachary Taylor 1849–1850
Millard Fillmore 1850–1853
Franklin Pierce 1853–1857
James Buchanan 1857–1861
Abraham Lincoln 1861–1865
Andrew Johnson 1865–1869
Ulysses S. Grant 1869–1877
Rutherford B. Hayes 1877–1881
James A. Garfield 1881

Chester A. Arthur 1881–1885
Grover Cleveland 1885–1889
Benjamin Harrison 1889–1893
Grover Cleveland 1893–1897
William McKinley 1897–1901
Theodore Roosevelt 1901–1909
William H. Taft 1909–1913
Woodrow Wilson 1913–1921
Warren G. Harding 1921–1923
Calvin Coolidge 1923–1929
Herbert Hoover 1929–1933
Franklin D. Roosevelt 1933–1945
Harry S Truman 1945–1953
Dwight D. Eisenhower 1953–1961
John F. Kennedy 1961–1963
Lyndon B. Johnson 1963–1969
Richard M. Nixon 1969–1974
Gerald R. Ford 1974–1977
Jimmy Carter 1977–1981
Ronald Reagan 1981–

Biographical Data — Presidents

Adams, John

Date of birth	Oct 30, 1735
Date of inauguration/age	Mar 4, 1797/61
Retirement from presidency/age	Mar 3, 1801/65
Date of death/age	Jul 4, 1826/96
Years of service/retirement	4y/25y 4m 1d

Adams, John Quincy

Date of birth	Jul 11, 1767
Date of inauguration/age	Mar 4, 1825/57
Retirement from presidency/age	Mar 3, 1829/61
Date of death/age	Feb 23, 1848/80
Years of service/retirement	4y/18y 11m 20d

Arthur, Chester A.

Date of birth	Oct 5, 1830
Date of inauguration/age	Sep 20, 1881/50
Retirement from presidency/age	Mar 3, 1885/53
Date of death/age	Nov 18, 1886/56
Years of service/retirement	3y 5m 11d/1y 8m 15d

Buchanan, James

Date of birth	Apr 23, 1791
Date of inauguration/age	Mar 4, 1857/65
Retirement from presidency/age	Mar 3, 1861/69
Date of death/age	Jun 1, 1868/77
Years of service/retirement	4y/7y 2m 28d

Carter, Jimmy

Date of birth	Oct 1, 1924
Date of inauguration/age	Jan 20, 1977/52
Retirement from presidency/age	Jan 20, 1981/56
Date of death/age	— — —
Years of service/retirement	4y/— — —

Cleveland, Grover

Date of birth	Mar 18, 1837
Date of inauguration/age	Mar 4, 1885/47,
	Mar 4, 1893/55
Retirement from presidency/age	Mar 3, 1889/51,
	Mar 3, 1897/59
Date of death/age	Jun 24, 1908/71
Years of service/retirement	4y/15y 3m 21d, 4y/11y
	3m 21d

Coolidge, Calvin

Date of birth	Jul 4, 1872
Date of inauguration/age	Aug 3, 1923/51
Retirement from presidency/age	Mar 3, 1929/57
Date of death/age	Jan 5, 1933/60
Years of service/retirement	5y 7m/3y 10m 2d

Eisenhower, Dwight D

Date of birth	Oct 14, 1890
Date of inauguration/age	Jan 20, 1953/62
Retirement from presidency/age	Jan 20, 1961/70
Date of death/age	Mar 28, 1969/78
Years of service/retirement	8y/8y 2m 8d

Fillmore, Millard

Date of birth	Jan 7, 1800
Date of inauguration/age	Jul 10, 1850/50
Retirement from presidency/age	Mar 3, 1853/53
Date of death/age	Mar 8, 1874/74
Years of service/retirement	2y 7m 21d/21y 5m

Ford, Gerald R.
Date of birth	Jul 14, 1913
Date of inauguration/age	Aug 9, 1974/61
Retirement from presidency/age	Jan 20, 1977/63
Date of death/age	— — —
Years of service/retirement	2y 5m 11d/— — —

Garfield, James A.
Date of birth	Nov 19, 1831
Date of inauguration/age	Mar 4, 1881/49
Retirement from presidency/age	Sep 19, 1881/49
Date of death/age	Sep 19, 1881/49
Years of service/retirement	6m 15d/0

Grant, Ulysses S.
Date of birth	Apr 27, 1822
Date of inauguration/age	Mar 4, 1869/46
Retirement from presidency/age	Mar 3, 1877/54
Date of death/age	Jul 23, 1885/63
Years of service/retirement	8y/8y 4m 20d

Harding, Warren G.
Date of birth	Nov 2, 1865
Date of inauguration/age	Mar 4, 1921/55
Retirement from presidency/age	Aug 2, 1923/57
Date of death/age	Aug 2, 1923/57
Years of service/retirement	2y 4m 28d/0

Harrison, Benjamin
Date of birth	Aug 20, 1833
Date of inauguration/age	Mar 4, 1889/55
Retirement from presidency/age	Mar 3, 1893/59
Date of death/age	Mar 13, 1901/67
Years of service/retirement	4y/8y 10d

Harrison, William Henry
Date of birth	Feb 9, 1773
Date of inauguration/age	Mar 4, 1841/68
Retirement from presidency/age	Apr 4, 1841/68
Date of death/age	Apr 4, 1841/68
Years of service/retirement	1m/0

Hayes, Rutherford B.
Date of birth	Oct 4, 1822
Date of inauguration/age	Mar 4, 1877/54
Retirement from presidency/age	Mar 3, 1881/58
Date of death/age	Jan 17, 1893/70
Years of service/retirement	4y/11y 10m 14d

Hoover, Herbert
Date of birth	Aug 10, 1874
Date of inauguration/age	Mar 4, 1929/54
Retirement from presidency/age	Mar 3, 1933/58
Date of death/age	Oct 20, 1964/90
Years of service/retirement	4y/31y 7m 17d

Jackson, Andrew
Date of birth	Mar 15, 1767
Date of inauguration/age	Mar 4, 1829/61
Retirement from presidency/age	Mar 3, 1837/69
Date of death/age	Jun 8, 1845/78
Years of service/retirement	8y/8y 3m 5d

Jefferson, Thomas
Date of birth	Apr 13, 1743
Date of inauguration/age	Mar 4, 1801/57
Retirement from presidency/age	Mar 3, 1809/65
Date of death/age	Jul 4, 1826/83
Years of service/retirement	8y/17y 4m 1d

Johnson, Andrew
Date of birth	Dec 29, 1808
Date of inauguration/age	Apr 15, 1865/56
Retirement from presidency/age	Mar 3, 1869/60
Date of death/age	Jul 31, 1875/66
Years of service/retirement	3y 10m 16d/6y 4m 28d

Johnson, Lyndon B.
Date of birth	Aug 27, 1908
Date of inauguration/age	Nov 22, 1963/55
Retirement from presidency/age	Jan 20, 1969/61
Date of death/age	Jan 22, 1973/65
Years of service/retirement	5y 1m 29d/4y 2d

Kennedy, John F.

Date of birth	May 29, 1917
Date of inauguration/age	Jan 20, 1961/43
Retirement from presidency/age	Nov 22, 1963/46
Date of death/age	Nov 22, 1963/46
Years of service/retirement	2y 10m 2d/0

Lincoln, Abraham

Date of birth	Feb 12, 1809
Date of inauguration/age	Mar 4, 1861/52
Retirement from presidency/age	Apr 15, 1865/56
Date of death/age	Apr 15, 1865/56
Years of service/retirement	4y 1m 11d/0

McKinley, William

Date of birth	Jan 29, 1843
Date of inauguration/age	Mar 4, 1897/54
Retirement from presidency/age	Sep 14, 1901/58
Date of death/age	Sep 14, 1901/58
Years of service/retirement	3y 6m 10d/0

Madison, James

Date of birth	Mar 16, 1751
Date of inauguration/age	Mar 4, 1809/57
Retirement from presidency/age	Mar 3, 1817/65
Date of death/age	Jun 28, 1836/85
Years of service/retirement	8y/19y 3m 25d

Monroe, James

Date of birth	Apr 28, 1758
Date of inauguration/age	Mar 4, 1817/58
Retirement from presidency/age	Mar 3, 1825/66
Date of death/age	Jul 4, 1831/73
Years of service/retirement	8y/6y 4m 1d

Nixon, Richard M.

Date of birth	Jan 9, 1913
Date of inauguration/age	Jan 20, 1969/56
Retirement from presidency/age	Aug 9, 1974/61
Date of death/age	— — —
Years of service/retirement	5y 6m 20d/— — —

Pierce, Franklin

Date of birth	Nov 23, 1804
Date of inauguration/age	Mar 4, 1853/48
Retirement from presidency/age	Mar 3, 1857/52
Date of death/age	Oct 8, 1869/64
Years of service/retirement	4y/12y 7m 5d

Polk, James K.

Date of birth	Nov 2, 1795
Date of inauguration/age	Mar 4, 1845/49
Retirement from presidency/age	Mar 3, 1849/53
Date of death/age	Jun 15, 1849/53
Years of service/retirement	4y/3m 12d

Reagan, Ronald

Date of birth	Feb 6, 1911
Date of inauguration/age	Jan 20, 1981/69
Retirement from presidency/age	— — —
Date of death/age	— — —
Years of service/retirement	— — —

Roosevelt, Franklin D.

Date of birth	Jan 30, 1882
Date of inauguration/age	Mar 4, 1933/51
Retirement from presidency/age	Apr 12, 1945/63
Date of death/age	Apr 12, 1945/63
Years of service/retirement	12y 1m 8d/0

Roosevelt, Theodore

Date of birth	Oct 27, 1858
Date of inauguration/age	Sep 14, 1901/42
Retirement from presidency/age	Mar 3, 1909/50
Date of death/age	Jan 6, 1919/60
Years of service/retirement	7y 5m 17d/9y 10m 3d

Taft, William H.

Date of birth	Sep 15, 1857
Date of inauguration/age	Mar 4, 1909/51
Retirement from presidency/age	Mar 3, 1913/55
Date of death/age	Mar 8, 1930/72
Years of service/retirement	4y/17y 5d

Taylor, Zachary
Date of birth .... Nov 24, 1784
Date of inauguration/age .... Mar 4, 1849/64
Retirement from presidency/age ..... Jul 9, 1850/65
Date of death/age .... Jul 9, 1850/65
Years of service/retirement 1y 4m 5d/0

Truman, Harry S
Date of birth .... May 8, 1884
Date of inauguration/age .... Apr 12, 1945/60
Retirement from presidency/age ..... Jan 20, 1953/68
Date of death/age .... Dec 26, 1972/88
Years of service/retirement 7y 9m 8d/19y 11m 6d

Tyler, John
Date of birth .... Mar 29, 1790
Date of inauguration/age .... Apr 6, 1841/51
Retirement from presidency/age ..... Mar 3, 1845/54
Date of death/age .... Jan 18, 1862/71
Years of service/retirement 4y 10m 25d/16y 10m 15d

Van Buren, Martin
Date of birth .... Dec 5, 1782
Date of inauguration/age .... Mar 4, 1837/54
Retirement from presidency/age ..... Mar 3, 1841/58
Date of death/age .... Jul 24, 1862/79
Years of service/retirement 4y/21y 4m 21d

Washington, George
Date of birth .... Feb 22, 1732
Date of inauguration/age .... Apr 30, 1789/57
Retirement from presidency/age ..... Mar 3, 1797/65
Date of death/age .... Dec 14, 1799/67
Years of service/retirement 7y 10m 3d/2y 9m 11d

Wilson, Woodrow
Date of birth .... Dec 28, 1856
Date of inauguration/age .... Mar 4, 1913/56
Retirement from presidency/age ..... Mar 3, 1921/64
Date of death/age .... Feb 3, 1924/67
Years of service/retirement 8y/2y 11m

Vice Presidential Succession

John Adams 1789–1797
Thomas Jefferson 1797–1801
Aaron Burr 1801–1805
George Clinton 1805–1812
Elbridge Gerry 1813–1814
Daniel D. Tompkins 1817–1825
John C. Calhoun 1825–1832
Martin Van Buren 1833–1837
Richard M. Johnson 1837–1841
John Tyler 1841
George M. Dallas 1845–1849
Millard Fillmore 1849–1850
William R. King 1853
John C. Breckinridge 1857–1861
Hannibal Hamlin 1861–1865
Andrew Johnson 1865
Schuyler Colfax 1869–1873
Henry Wilson 1873–1875
William A. Wheeler 1877–1881
Chester A. Arthur 1881
Thomas A. Hendricks 1885
Levi P. Morton 1889–1893

Adlai E. Stevenson 1893–1897
Garrett A. Hobart 1897–1899
Theodore Roosevelt 1901
Charles W. Fairbanks 1905–1909
James S. Sherman 1909–1912
Thomas R. Marshall 1913–1921
Calvin Coolidge 1921–1923
Charles G. Dawes 1925–1929
Charles Curtis 1929–1933
John N. Garner 1933–1941
Henry A. Wallace 1941–1945
Harry S Truman 1945
Alben W. Barkley 1949–1953
Richard M. Nixon 1953–1961
Lyndon B. Johnson 1961–1963
Hubert H. Humphrey 1965–1969
Spiro T. Agnew 1969–1973
Gerald R. Ford 1973–1974
Nelson A. Rockefeller 1974–1977
Walter F. Mondale 1977–1981
George H. Bush 1981–

Biographical Data—Vice Presidents

Adams, John

Date of birth	Oct 30, 1735
Date of inauguration/age	Apr 21, 1789/53
Retirement from office/age.........	Mar 3, 1797/61
Date of death/age	Jul 4, 1826/90
Years of service/retirement	7y 10m 10d/29y 4m 1d

Agnew, Spiro T.

Date of birth	Nov 9, 1918
Date of inauguration/age	Jan 20, 1969/50
Retirement from office/age.........	Oct 10, 1973/54
Date of death/age	— — —
Years of service/retirement	4y 8m 20d/— — —

Arthur, Chester A.

Date of birth	Oct 5, 1830
Date of inauguration/age	Mar 4, 1881/50
Retirement from office/age.........	Sep 19, 1881/50
Date of death/age	Nov 18, 1886/56
Years of service/retirement	6m 15d/5y 1m 29d

Barkley, Alben W.

Date of birth	Nov 24, 1877
Date of inauguration/age	Jan 20, 1949/71
Retirement from office/age.........	Jan 20, 1953/75
Date of death/age	Apr 30, 1956/78
Years of service/retirement	4y/3y 3m 10d

Breckinridge, John C.

Date of birth	Jan 21, 1821
Date of inauguration/age	Mar 4, 1857/36
Retirement from office/age	Mar 3, 1861/40
Date of death/age	May 17, 1875/54
Years of service/retirement	4y/14y 2m 14d

Burr, Aaron

Date of birth	Feb 6, 1756
Date of inauguration/age	Mar 4, 1801/45
Retirement from office/age	Mar 3, 1805/49
Date of death/age	Sep 14, 1836/80
Years of service/retirement	4y/31y 6m 11d

Bush, George H.

Date of birth	Jun 12, 1924
Date of inauguration/age	Jan 20, 1981/56
Retirement from office/age	— — —
Date of death/age	— — —
Years of service/retirement	— — —

Calhoun, John C.

Date of birth	Mar 18, 1782
Date of inauguration/age	Mar 4, 1825/42
Retirement from office/age	Dec 28, 1832/50
Date of death/age	Mar 31, 1850/68
Years of service/retirement	7y 9m 24d/17y 3m 3d

Clinton, George

Date of birth	Jul 26, 1739
Date of inauguration/age	Mar 4, 1805/65
Retirement from office/age	Apr 20, 1812/72
Date of death/age	Apr 20, 1812/72
Years of service/retirement	7y 1m 16d/0

Colfax, Schuyler

Date of birth	Mar 23, 1823
Date of inauguration/age	Mar 4, 1869/45
Retirement from office/age	Mar 3, 1873/49
Date of death/age	Jan 13, 1885/61
Years of service/retirement	4y/11y 10m 10d

Coolidge, Calvin

Date of birth	Jul 4, 1872
Date of inauguration/age	Mar 4, 1921/48
Retirement from office/age.........	Aug 3, 1923/51
Date of death/age	Jan 5, 1933/60
Years of service/retirement	2y 5m/9y 5m 2d

Curtis, Charles

Date of birth	Jan 25, 1860
Date of inauguration/age	Mar 4, 1929/69
Retirement from office/age.........	Mar 3, 1933/73
Date of death/age	Feb 8, 1936/76
Years of service/retirement	4y/2y 11m 5d

Dallas, George M.

Date of birth	Jul 10, 1792
Date of inauguration/age	Mar 4, 1845/52
Retirement from office/age.........	Mar 3, 1849/56
Date of death/age	Dec 31, 1864/72
Years of service/retirement	4y/15y 9m 28d

Dawes, Charles G.

Date of birth	Aug 27, 1865
Date of inauguration/age	Mar 4, 1925/59
Retirement from office/age.........	Mar 3, 1929/63
Date of death/age	Apr 23, 1951/85
Years of service/retirement	4y/22y 1m 20d

Fairbanks, Charles W.

Date of birth	May 11, 1852
Date of inauguration/age	Mar 4, 1905/52
Retirement from office/age.........	Mar 3, 1909/56
Date of death/age	Jun 4, 1918/66
Years of service/retirement	4y/9y 3m 1d

Fillmore, Millard

Date of birth	Jan 7, 1800
Date of inauguration/age	Mar 4, 1849/49
Retirement from office/age.........	Jul 9, 1850/50
Date of death/age	Mar 8, 1874/74
Years of service/retirement	1y 4m 5d/23y 7m 27d

Ford, Gerald R.

Date of birth	Jul 14, 1913
Date of inauguration/age	Dec 6, 1973/60
Retirement from office/age.	Aug 9, 1974/61
Date of death/age	— — —
Years of service/retirement	8m 3d/ — — —

Garner, John N.

Date of birth	Nov 22, 1868
Date of inauguration/age	Mar 4, 1933/64
Retirement from office/age.	Jan 19, 1941/72
Date of death/age	Nov 7, 1967/98
Years of service/retirement	7y 10m 15d/26y 9m 19d

Gerry, Elbridge

Date of birth	Jul 17, 1744
Date of inauguration/age	Mar 4, 1813/68
Retirement from office/age.	Nov 23, 1813/70
Date of death/age	Nov 23, 1814/70
Years of service/retirement	1y 8m 19d/0

Hamlin, Hannibal

Date of birth	Aug 27, 1809
Date of inauguration/age	Mar 4, 1861/51
Retirement from office/age.	Mar 3, 1865/55
Date of death/age	Jul 4, 1891/81
Years of service/retirement	4y/26y 4m 1d

Hendricks, Thomas A.

Date of birth	Sep 7, 1819
Date of inauguration/age	Mar 4, 1885/65
Retirement from office/age.	Nov 25, 1885/66
Date of death/age	Nov 25, 1885/66
Years of service/retirement	7m 21d/0

Hobart, Garrett A.

Date of birth	Jun 3, 1844
Date of inauguration/age	Mar 4, 1897/52
Retirement from office/age.	Nov 21, 1899/55
Date of death/age	Nov 21, 1899/55
Years of service/retirement	2y 8m 17d/0

Humphrey, Hubert H.
Date of birth	May 27, 1911
Date of inauguration/age	Jan 20, 1965/53
Retirement from office/age.........	Jan 20, 1969/57
Date of death/age	Jan 13, 1978/66
Years of service/retirement	4y/8y 11m 24d

Jefferson, Thomas
Date of birth	Apr 13, 1743
Date of inauguration/age	Mar 4, 1797/53
Retirement from office/age.........	Mar 3, 1801/57
Date of death/age	Jul 4, 1826/83
Years of service/retirement	4y/25y 4m 1d

Johnson, Andrew
Date of birth	Dec 29, 1808
Date of inauguration/age	Mar 4, 1865/56
Retirement from office/age.........	Apr 15, 1865/56
Date of death/age	Jul 31, 1875/66
Years of service/retirement	1m 11d/10y 3m 16d

Johnson, Lyndon B.
Date of birth	Aug 27, 1908
Date of inauguration/age	Jan 20, 1961/52
Retirement from office/age.........	Nov 22, 1963/55
Date of death/age	Jan 22, 1973/64
Years of service/retirement	2y 10m 2d/9y 2m

Johnson, Richard M.
Date of birth	Oct 17, 1780
Date of inauguration/age	Mar 4, 1837/56
Retirement from office/age.........	Mar 3, 1841/60
Date of death/age	Nov 19, 1850/70
Years of service/retirement	4y/9y 8m 16d

King, William R.
Date of birth	Apr 7, 1786
Date of inauguration/age	Mar 4, 1853/66
Retirement from office/age.........	Apr 18, 1853/67
Date of death/age	Apr 18, 1853/67
Years of service/retirement	1m 14d/0

Marshall, Thomas R.
Date of birth	Mar 14, 1854
Date of inauguration/age	Mar 4, 1913/58
Retirement from office/age.	Mar 3, 1921/66
Date of death/age	Jun 1, 1925/71
Years of service/retirement	8y/4y 2m 28d

Mondale, Walter F.
Date of birth	Jan 5, 1928
Date of inauguration/age	Jan 20, 1977/49
Retirement from office/age.	Jan 20, 1981/53
Date of death/age	— — —
Years of service/retirement	4y/— — —

Morton, Levi P.
Date of birth	May 16, 1824
Date of inauguration/age	Mar 4, 1889/64
Retirement from office/age.	Mar 3, 1893/68
Date of death/age	May 16, 1920/96
Years of service/retirement	4y/27y 2m 13d

Nixon, Richard M.
Date of birth	Jan 9, 1913
Date of inauguration/age	Jan 20, 1953/40
Retirement from office/age.	Jan 20, 1961/48
Date of death/age	— — —
Years of service/retirement	8y/— — —

Rockefeller, Nelson A.
Date of birth	Jul 8, 1908
Date of inauguration/age	Dec 19, 1974/66
Retirement from office/age.	Jan 20, 1977/68
Date of death/age	Jan 26, 1979/70
Years of service/retirement	2y 1m 1d/2y 6d

Roosevelt, Theodore
Date of birth	Oct 27, 1858
Date of inauguration/age	Mar 4, 1901/42
Retirement from office/age.	Sep 14, 1901/42
Date of death/age	Jan 6, 1919/60
Years of service/retirement	6m 10d/17y 3m 23d

Sherman, James S.

Date of birth	Oct 24, 1855
Date of inauguration/age	Mar 4, 1909/53
Retirement from office/age	Oct 30, 1912/57
Date of death/age	Oct 30, 1912/57
Years of service/retirement	3y 7m 26d/0

Stevenson, Adlai E.

Date of birth	Oct 23, 1835
Date of inauguration/age	Mar 4, 1893/57
Retirement from office/age	Mar 3, 1897/61
Date of death/age	Jun 14, 1914/78
Years of service/retirement	4y/17y 3m 11d

Tompkins, Daniel D.

Date of birth	Jun 21, 1774
Date of inauguration/age	Mar 4, 1817/42
Retirement from office/age	Mar 3, 1825/50
Date of death/age	Jun 11, 1825/50
Years of service/retirement	8y/3m 8d

Truman, Harry S

Date of birth	May 8, 1884
Date of inauguration/age	Jan 20, 1945/60
Retirement from office/age	Apr 12, 1945/60
Date of death/age	Dec 26, 1972/88
Years of service/retirement	2m 23d/27y 8m 14d

Tyler, John

Date of birth	Mar 29, 1790
Date of inauguration/age	Mar 4, 1841/50
Retirement from office/age	Apr 6, 1841/51
Date of death/age	Jan 18, 1862/71
Years of service/retirement	1m 2d/20y 9m 12d

Van Buren, Martin

Date of birth	Dec 5, 1782
Date of inauguration/age	Mar 4, 1833/50
Retirement from office/age	Mar 3, 1837/54
Date of death/age	Jul 24, 1862/79
Years of service/retirement	4y/25y 4m 21d

Wallace, Henry A.

Date of birth	Oct 7, 1888
Date of inauguration/age	Jan 20, 1941/52
Retirement from office/age..........	Jan 20, 1945/56
Date of death/age	Nov 18, 1965/77
Years of service/retirement	4y/20y 10m

Wheeler, William A.

Date of birth	Jun 30, 1819
Date of inauguration/age	Mar 4, 1877/57
Retirement from office/age..........	Mar 3, 1881/61
Date of death/age	Jun 4, 1887/67
Years of service/retirement	4y/6y 3m 1d

Wilson, Henry

Date of birth	Feb 16, 1812
Date of inauguration/age	Mar 4, 1873/61
Retirement from office/age..........	Nov 22, 1875/63
Date of death/age	Nov 22, 1875/63
Years of service/retirement	2y 3m 18d/0

Cabinet Succession

Secretary of State

Thomas Jefferson 1789–1794
Edmund Randolph 1794–1795
Timothy Pickering 1795–1800
John Marshall 1800–1801
James Madison 1801–1809
Robert Smith 1809–1811
James Monroe 1811–1817
John Quincy Adams 1817–1825
Henry Clay 1825–1829
Martin Van Buren 1829–1831
Edward Livingston 1831–1833
Louis Mclane 1833–1834
John Forsyth 1834–1841
Daniel Webster 1841–1843
Abel P. Upshur 1843–1844
John C. Calhoun 1844–1845
James Buchanan 1845–1849
John M. Clayton 1849–1850
Daniel Webster 1850–1852
Edward Everett 1852–1853
William L. Marcy 1853–1857
Lewis Cass 1857–1860
Jeremiah S. Black 1860–1861
William H. Seward 1861–1869
Elihu B. Washburne 1869
Hamilton Fish 1869–1877
William M. Evarts 1877–1881
James G. Blaine 1881
Frederick T. Frelinghuysen 1881–1885
Thomas F. Bayard 1885–1889

James G. Blaine 1889–1892
John W. Foster 1892–1893
Walter Q. Gresham 1893–1895
Richard Olney 1895–1897
John Sherman 1897–1898
William R. Day 1898
John Hay 1898–1905
Elihu Root 1905–1909
Robert Bacon 1909
Philander C. Knox 1909–1913
William J. Bryan 1913–1915
Robert Lansing 1915–1920
Bainbridge Colby 1920–1921
Charles Evans Hughes 1921–1925
Frank B. Kellogg 1925–1929
Henry L. Stimson 1929–1933
Cordell Hull 1933–1944
Edward R. Stettinius 1944–1945
James F. Byrnes 1945–1947
George C. Marshall 1947–1949
Dean G. Acheson 1949–1953
John Foster Dulles 1953–1959
Christian A. Herter 1959–1961
Dean Rusk 1961–1969
William P. Rogers 1969–1973
Henry A. Kissinger 1973–1977
Cyrus R. Vance 1977–1980
Edmund S. Muskie 1980–1981
Alexander M. Haig, Jr. 1981–1982
George P. Shultz 1982–

Secretary of the Treasury

Alexander Hamilton 1789–1795
Oliver Wolcott, Jr. 1795–1800
Samuel Dexter 1801
Albert Gallatin 1801–1814
George W. Campbell 1814
Alexander J. Dallas 1814–1816
William H. Crawford 1816–1825
Richard Rush 1825–1829
Samuel D. Ingham 1829–1831
Louis McLane 1831–1833
William J. Duane 1833
Roger B. Taney 1833–1834
Levi Woodbury 1834–1841
Thomas Ewing 1841
Walter Forward 1841–1843
John C. Spencer 1843–1844
George M. Bibb 1844–1845
Robert J. Walker 1845–1849
William M. Meredith 1849–1850
Thomas Corwin 1850–1853
James Guthrie 1853–1857
Howell Cobb 1857–1860
Phillip F. Thomas 1860–1861
John A. Dix 1861
Salmon P. Chase 1861–1864
William P. Fessenden 1864–1865
Hugh McCulloch 1865–1869
George S. Boutwell 1869–1873
William A. Richardson 1873–1874
Benjamin H. Bristow 1874–1876
Lot M. Morrill 1876–1877
John Sherman 1877–1881
William Windom 1881
Charles J. Folger 1881–1884

Walter Q. Gresham 1884
Hugh McCulloch 1884–1885
Daniel Manning 1885–1887
Charles S. Fairchild 1887–1889
William Windom 1889–1891
Charles Foster 1891–1893
John G. Carlisle 1893–1897
Lyman J. Gage 1897–1902
Leslie M. Shaw 1902–1907
George B. Cortelyou 1907–1909
Franklin McVeagh 1909–1913
William G. McAdoo 1913–1918
Carter Glass 1918–1920
David F. Houston 1920–1921
Andrew W. Mellon 1921–1932
Ogden L. Mills 1932–1933
William H. Woodin 1933
Henry Morgenthau, Jr. 1934–1945
Frederick M. Vinson 1945–1946
John W. Snyder 1946–1953
George M. Humphrey 1953–1957
Robert B. Anderson 1957–1961
C. Douglas Dillon 1961–1965
Henry H. Fowler 1965–1968
Joseph W. Barr 1968–1969
David M. Kennedy 1969–1971
John B. Connally 1971–1973
George P. Shultz 1972–1974
William E. Simon 1974–1977
W. Michael Blumenthal 1977–1979
G. William Miller 1979–1981
Donald T. Regan 1981–1985
James A. Baker, III 1985–

Secretary of War

Henry Knox 1789–1795
Timothy Pickering 1795

James McHenry 1796–1800
Samuel Dexter 1800

Henry Dearborn 1801–1809
William Eustis 1809–1812
John Armstrong 1813–1814
James Monroe 1814–1815
William H. Crawford 1815–1816
John C. Calhoun 1817–1825
James Barbour 1825–1828
Peter B. Porter 1828–1829
John H. Eaton 1829–1831
Lewis Cass 1831–1836
Joel R. Poinsett 1837–1841
John Bell 1841
John C. Spencer 1841–1843
James M. Porter 1843–1844
William Wilkins 1844–1845
William L. Marcy 1845–1849
George W. Crawford 1844–1850
Charles M. Conrad 1850–1853
Jefferson Davis 1853–1857
John B. Floyd 1857–1861
Simon Cameron 1861–1862
Edwin M. Stanton 1862, 1867
Edwin M. Stanton 1868
John M. Schofield 1868–1869
John A. Rawlins 1869
William T. Sherman 1869
William W. Belknap 1869–1876

Alphonso Taft 1876
James D. Cameron 1876–1877
George W. McCrary 1877–1879
Alexander Ramsey 1879–1881
Robert T. Lincoln 1881–1885
William C. Endicott 1885–1889
Redfield Proctor 1889–1891
Stephen B. Elkins 1891–1893
Daniel S. Lamont 1893–1897
Russell A. Alger 1897–1899
Elihu Root 1899–1904
William H. Taft 1904–1908
Luke E. Wright 1908–1909
Jacob G. Dickinson 1909–1911
Henry L. Stimson 1911–1913
Lindley M. Garrison 1913–1916
Newton D. Baker 1916–1921
John W. Weeks 1921–1925
Dwight F. Davis 1925–1929
James W. Good 1929
Patrick J. Hurley 1929–1933
George H. Dern 1933–1936
Harry H. Woodring 1937–1940
Henry L. Stimson 1940–1945
Robert P. Patterson 1945–1947
Kenneth C. Royall 1947

Attorney General

Edmund Randolph 1789–1794
William Bradford 1794–1795
Charles Lee 1795–1801
Levi Lincoln 1801–1804
John Breckenridge 1805–1806
Caesar A. Rodney 1807–1811
William Pinkney 1811–1814
Richard Rush 1814–1817
William Wirt 1817–1829
John M. Berrien 1829–1831
Roger B. Taney 1831–1833

Benjamin F. Butler 1833–1837
Felix Grundy 1838–1840
Henry D. Gilpin 1840–1841
John J. Crittenden 1841
Hugh S. Legare 1841–1843
John Nelson 1843–1845
John Y. Mason 1845–1846
Nathan Clifford 1846–1848
Isaac Toucey 1848–1849
Reverdy Johnson 1849–1850
John J. Crittenden 1850–1853

Caleb Cushing 1853-1857
Jeremiah S. Black 1857-1860
Edwin M. Stanton 1860-1861
Edward Bates 1861-1864
James Speed 1864-1866
Henry Stanbery 1866-1868
William M. Evarts 1868-1869
Ebenezer R. Hoar 1869-1870
Amos T. Akerman 1870-1872
George H. Williams 1871-1875
Edward Pierrepont 1875-1876
Alphonso Taft 1876-1877
Charles Devens 1877-1881
Wayne McVeagh 1881
Benjamin H. Brewster 1881-1885
Augustus H. Garland 1885-1889
William H.H. Miller 1889-1893
Richard Olney 1893-1895
Judson Harmon 1895-1897
Joseph McKenna 1897-1898
John W. Griggs 1898-1901
Philander C. Knox 1901-1904
William H. Moody 1904-1906
Charles J. Bonaparte 1906-1909
George W. Wickersham 1909-1913
J.C. McReynolds 1913-1914

Thomas W. Gregory 1914-1919
A. Mitchell Palmer 1919-1921
Harry M. Daugherty 1921-1924
Harlan F. Stone 1924-1925
John G. Sargent 1925-1929
William D. Mitchell 1929-1933
Homer S. Cummings 1933-1939
Frank Murphy 1939-1940
Robert H. Jackson 1940-1941
Francis Biddle 1941-1945
Thomas C. Clarke 1945-1949
J. Howard McGrath 1949-1953
Herbert Brownell, Jr. 1953-1958
William P. Rogers 1958-1961
Robert F. Kennedy 1961-1965
Nicholas Katzenbach 1965-1967
Ramsey Clark 1967-1969
John N. Mitchell 1969-1972
Richard G. Kleindienst 1972-1973
Elliot L. Richardson 1973-1974
William B. Saxbe 1974-1975
Edward H. Levi 1975-1977
Griffin B. Bell 1977-1979
Benjamin R. Civiletti 1979-1981
William F. Smith 1981-

Postmaster General

Samuel Osgood 1789-1791
Timothy Pickering 1791-1795
Joseph Habersham 1795-1801
Gideon Granger 1801-1814
Return J. Meigs, Jr. 1814-1823
John McLean 1823-1829
William T. Barry 1829-1835
Amos Kendall 1835-1840
John M. Niles 1840-1841
Francis Granger 1841
Charles A. Wickliffe 1841-1845
Cave Johnson 1845-1849

Jacob Collamer 1849-1850
Nathan K. Hall 1850-1852
Samuel D. Hubbard 1852-1853
James Campbell 1853-1857
Aaron V. Brown 1857-1859
Joseph Holt 1859-1860
Horatio King 1861
Montgomery Blair 1861-1864
William Dennison 1864-1866
Alexander W. Randall 1866-1869
John A.J. Creswell 1869-1874
James W. Marshall 1874

Marshall Jewell 1874–1876
James N. Tyner 1876–1877
David M. Key 1877–1880
Horace Maynard 1880–1881
Thomas L. James 1881–1882
Timothy O. Howe 1882–1883
Walter Q. Gresham 1883–1884
Frank Hatton 1884–1885
William F. Vilas 1885–1888
Donald M. Dickinson 1888–1889
John Wanamaker 1889–1893
Wilson S. Bissell 1893–1895
William L. Wilson 1895–1897
James A. Gary 1897–1898
Charles E. Smith 1898–1902
Henry C. Payne 1902–1904
Robert J. Wynne 1904–1905
George B. Cortelyou 1905–1907

George von L. Meyer 1907–1909
Frank H. Hitchcock 1909–1913
Albert S. Burleson 1913–1921
Will H. Hays 1921–1922
Hubert Work 1922–1923
Harry S. New 1923–1929
Walter F. Brown 1929–1933
James A. Farley 1933–1940
Frank C. Walker 1940–1945
Robert E. Hannegan 1945–1947
Jesse M. Donaldson 1947–1953
A.E. Summerfield 1953–1961
J. Edward Day 1961–1963
John A. Gronouski 1963–1965
Lawrence F. O'Brien 1965–1968
W. Marvin Watson 1968–1969
Winton M. Blount 1969–1970

Secretary of the Navy

Benjamin Stoddert 1798–1801
Robert Smith 1801–1809
Paul Hamilton 1809–1812
William Jones 1813–1814
Benjamin W. Crowninshield 1815–1818
Smith Thompson 1819–1823
Samuel L. Southard 1823–1829
John Branch 1829–1831
Levi Woodbury 1831–1834
Mahlon Dickerson 1834–1838
James K. Paulding 1838–1841
George E. Badger 1841
Abel P. Upshur 1841–1843
David Henshaw 1843–1844
Thomas W. Gilmer 1844
John Y. Mason 1844–1845
George Bancroft 1845–1846
John Y. Mason 1846–1849
William B. Preston 1849–1850

William A. Graham 1850–1852
John P. Kennedy 1852–1853
James C. Dobbin 1953–1857
Isaac Toucey 1857–1861
Gideon Welles 1861–1869
Adolph E. Borie 1869
George M. Robeson 1869–1877
Richard W. Thompson 1877–1880
Nathan Goff, Jr. 1881
William H. Hunt 1881–1882
William E. Chandler 1882–1885
William C. Whitney 1885–1889
Benjamin F. Tracy 1889–1893
Hilary A. Herbert 1893–1897
John D. Long 1897–1902
William H. Moody 1902–1904
Paul Morton 1904–1905
Charles J. Bonaparte 1905–1906
Victor H. Metcalf 1906–1908
Truman H. Newberry 1908–1909

George von L. Meyer 1909–1913
Josephus Daniels 1913–1921
Edwin Denby 1921–1924
Curtis D. Wilbur 1924–1929
Charles F. Adams 1929–1933

Claude A. Swanson 1933–1939
Charles Edison 1940
Frank Knox 1940–1944
James V. Forrestal 1944–1947

Secretary of the Interior

Thomas Ewing 1849–1850
Thomas M.T. McKennan 1850
Alex H.H. Stuart 1850–1853
Robert McClelland 1853–1857
Jacob Thompson 1857–1861
Caleb B. Smith 1861–1862
John P. Usher 1863–1865
James Harlan 1865–1866
Orville H. Browning 1866–1869
Jacob D. Cox 1869–1870
Columbus O. Delano 1870–1875
Zachariah Chandler 1875–1877
Carl Schurz 1877–1881
Samuel J. Kirkwood 1881–1882
Henry M. Teller 1882–1885
Lucius Q.C. Lamar 1885–1888
William F. Vilas 1888–1889
John W. Noble 1889–1893
Hoke Smith 1893–1896
David R. Francis 1896–1897
Cornelius N. Bliss 1897–1899
Ethan A. Hitchcock 1899–1907
James R. Garfield 1907–1909

Richard A. Ballinger 1909–1911
Walter L. Fisher 1911–1913
Franklin K. Kane 1913–1920
John B. Payne 1920–1921
Albert B. Fall 1921–1923
Hubert Work 1923–1928
Roy O. West 1929
Ray L. Wilbur 1929–1933
Harold L. Ickes 1933–1946
Julius A. Krug 1946–1949
Oscar L. Chapman 1950–1953
Douglas McKay 1953–1956
Fred A. Seaton 1956–1961
Stewart L. Udall 1961–1969
Walter J. Hickel 1969–1971
Rogers C.B. Morton 1971–1975
Stanley K. Hathaway 1975
Thomas S. Kleppe 1975–1977
Cecil D. Andrus 1977–1981
James G. Watt 1981–1983
William P. Clark 1983–1985
Donald P. Hodel 1985–

Secretary of Agriculture

Norman J. Colman 1889
Jeremiah M. Rusk 1889–1893
J. Sterling Morton 1893–1897

James Wilson 1897–1913
David F. Houston 1913–1920
Edwin T. Meredith 1920–1921

Henry C. Wallace 1921–1924
Howard M. Gore 1924–1925
William M. Jardine 1925–1929
Arthur M. Hyde 1929–1933
Henry A. Wallace 1933–1940
Claude R. Wickard 1940–1945
Clinton P. Anderson 1945–1948
Charles F. Brannan 1948–1953

Ezra T. Benson 1953–1961
Orville L. Freeman 1961–1969
Clifford M. Hardin 1969–1971
Earl L. Butz 1971–1976
John A. Knebel 1976–1977
Robert Bergland 1977–1981
John R. Block 1981–

Secretary of Commerce and Labor

George B. Cortelyou 1903–1904
Victor H. Metcalf 1904–1906

Oscar S. Straus 1906–1909
Charles Nagel 1909–1913

Secretary of Commerce

William C. Redfield 1913–1919
Joshua W. Alexander 1919–1921
Herbert C. Hoover 1921–1928
William F. Whiting 1928–1929
Robert P. Lamont 1929–1932
Roy D. Chapin 1932–1933
Daniel C. Roper 1933–1938
Harry L. Hopkins 1939–1940
Jesse Jones 1940–1945
Henry A. Wallace 1945–1946
William A. Harriman 1947–1948
Charles Sawyer 1948–1953
Sinclair Weeks 1953–1958
Lewis L. Strauss 1958–1959

Frederick H. Mueller 1959–1961
Luther H. Hodges 1961–1965
John T. Connor 1965–1967
Alex B. Trowbridge 1967–1968
Cyrus R. Smith 1968–1969
Maurice H. Stans 1969–1972
Peter G. Peterson 1972–1973
Frederick B. Dent 1973–1975
Rogers C.B. Morton 1975
Elliot L. Richardson 1975–1977
Juanita M. Kreps 1977–1979
Philip M. Klutznik 1979–1981
Malcolm Baldridge 1981–

Secretary of Labor

William B. Wilson 1913–1921
James J. Davis 1921–1930
William N. Doak 1930–1933
Frances Perkins 1933–1945
Lewis B. Schwellenbach 1945–1948
Maurice J. Tobin 1948–1953
Martin P. Durkin 1953
James P. Mitchell 1953–1961
Arthur J. Goldberg 1961–1962

W. Willard Wirtz 1962–1969
George P. Shultz 1969–1970
James D. Hodgson 1970–1973
Peter J. Brennan 1973–1975
John T. Dunlop 1975–1976
W.J. Usery, Jr. 1976–1977
F. Ray Marshall 1977–1981
Raymond J. Donovan 1981–

Secretary of Defense

James V. Forrestal 1947–1949
Louis A. Johnson 1949–1950
George C. Marshall 1950–1951
Robert A. Lovett 1951–1953
Charles E. Wilson 1953–1957
Neil H. McElroy 1957–1961
Robert S. McNamara 1961–1968

Clark M. Clifford 1968–1969
Melvin R. Laird 1969–1973
Elliot L. Richardson 1973
James R. Schlesinger 1973–1975
Donald H. Rumsfeld 1975–1977
Harold Brown 1977–1981
Caspar W. Weinberger 1981–

Secretary of Health, Education and Welfare

Oveta C. Hobby 1953–1955
Marion B. Folsom 1955–1958
Arthur S. Flemming 1958–1961
Abraham A. Ribicoff 1961–1962
Anthony J. Celebrezze 1962–1965
John W. Gardner 1965–1968
Wilbur J. Cohen 1968–1969

Robert H. Finch 1969–1970
Elliot L. Richardson 1970–1973
Caspar W. Weinberger 1973–1975
Forrest D. Mathews 1975–1977
Joseph A. Califano, Jr. 1977–1979
Patricia R. Harris 1979

Secretary of Housing
and Urban Development

Robert C. Weaver 1966–1969
Robert C. Wood 1969
George W. Romney 1969–1973
James T. Lynn 1973–1975

Carla A. Hills 1975–1977
Patricia R. Harris 1977–1979
Moon Landrieu 1979–1981
Samuel R. Pierce, Jr. 1981–

Secretary of Transportation

Alan S. Boyd 1967–1969
John A. Volpe 1969–1973
Claude S. Brinegar 1973–1975
William T. Coleman, Jr. 1975–1977

Brock Adams 1977–1979
Neil E. Goldschmidt 1979–1981
Andrew L. Lewis, Jr. 1981–1982
Elizabeth H. Dole 1982–

Secretary of Energy

James R. Schlesinger 1977–1979
Robert W. Duncan, Jr. 1979–1981
James B. Edwards 1981–1982

Donald P. Hodel 1982–1985
John S. Herrington 1985–

Secretary of Health
and Human Services

Patricia R. Harris 1979–1981
Richard S. Schweiker 1981–1983

Margaret M. Heckler 1983–

Secretary of Education

Shirley Hufstedler 1979–1981   William J. Bennett 1985–
Terrel Bell 1981–1985

Cabinet Office Summary

Department of State — Originally created by an act of Congress on July 27, 1789 as the Department of Foreign Affairs, the name of the department was changed to the Department of State on September 15, 1789.

Department of War — The War Department was created by Congress on August 7, 1789. On September 18, 1947 the War Department became the Department of the Army, and the Departments of the Army, Navy, and Air Force became branches of the Department of Defense.

Department of the Treasury — The Treasury Department was created by Congress on September 2, 1789.

Post Office Department — The Post Office Department was originally established as a branch of the Treasury Department on September 22, 1789. The Postmaster General was made a member of the president's cabinet on March 9, 1829. The Postal Reorganization Act of 1970 changed the organization to the U.S. Postal Service, and from July 1, 1970 the Postmaster General was no longer a member of the cabinet.

Office of Attorney General — The attorney general's office was organized on September 24, 1789. The Justice Department was created by Congress on June 22, 1870.

Navy Department — The Navy Department was created on April 30, 1798. The Navy Department became one of the branches of the Department of Defense on September 18, 1947. The Secretary of the Navy became a non-cabinet official on that date, though all three military departments — Army, Navy, and Air Force — are represented in the Cabinet by the Secretary of Defense.

Department of the Interior — The Interior Department was created by Congress on March 3, 1849.

Department of Agriculture — The Agriculture Department was created by Congress on May 15, 1862, but the Department was not at first represented in the president's cabinet. The Secretary of Agriculture became a member of the Cabinet on February 8, 1889.

Department of Commerce and Labor—The Commerce and Labor Department was created by Congress on February 14, 1903. The department was divided into separate departments of Commerce and Labor on March 4, 1913.

Department of Commerce—The Commerce Department was a subdivision of the Commerce and Labor Department until March 4, 1913 when the departments were separated and the Secretary of Commerce was commissioned as a separate Cabinet post.

Department of Labor—The Labor Department was a part of the Commerce and Labor Department until March 4, 1913 when the dual department was divided into two separate offices and the Secretary of Labor became an individual Cabinet officer.

Department of Defense—The Defense Department was created on September 18, 1947 to act as a unifying office to oversee the interests of the Army, Navy, and Air Force. The War Department became the Department of the Army, and it and the Department of the Navy, along with the new Department of the Air Force, became branches of the Department of Defense.

Department of Health, Education and Welfare—The department was created on April 11, 1953. Twenty-six years later, on September 27, 1979, the bureau was divided into the departments of Education and Health and Human Services.

Department of Housing and Urban Development—HUD was created by Congress on September 9, 1965.

Department of Transportation—The Transportation Department was created by Congress on October 15, 1966.

Department of Energy—The Energy Department was created by Congress on August 4, 1977.

Department of Health and Human Services—The Health and Human Services Department was created by Congress on September 27, 1979 when the Department of Health, Education and Welfare was divided into the Department of Health and Human Services and the Department of Education.

Department of Education—The Education Department was created by Congress on September 27, 1979, when HEW was divided into two separate departments, both represented by officers in the president's Cabinet.

Biographical Data— Cabinet Members

Acheson, Dean G.   **ST**
Date of birth .... Apr 11, 1893
Date of appointment/age .... Jan 19, 1949/55
Assumed office/age .... Jan 21, 1949/55
Left office/age .... Jan 20, 1953/59
Date of death/age .... Oct 12, 1971/78
Cabinet service 4y

Adams, Brockman   **TR**
Date of birth .... Jan 13, 1927
Date of appointment/age .... Dec 15, 1976/49
Assumed office/age .... Jan 21, 1977/50
Left office/age .... Jul 21, 1979/52
Date of death/age .... — — —
Cabinet service 2y 6m

Adams, Charles F.   **NV**
Date of birth .... Aug 2, 1866
Date of appointment/age .... Mar 5, 1929/62
Assumed office/age .... Mar 5, 1929/62
Left office/age .... Mar 3, 1933/66
Date of death/age .... Jun 11, 1954/87
Cabinet service 3y 11m 28d

Adams, John Q.   **ST**
Date of birth .... Jul 11, 1767
Date of appointment/age .... Mar 5, 1817/49
Assumed office/age .... Sep 22, 1817/50
Left office/age .... Mar 3, 1825/57
Date of death/age .... Feb 23, 1848/80
Cabinet service 7y 5m 9d

Akerman, Amos T.   **AT**
Date of birth ....   Feb 23, 1821
Date of appointment/age ....   Jun 23, 1870/49
Assumed office/age ....   Jul 8, 1870/49
Left office/age ....   Jan 9, 1872/50
Date of death/age ....   Dec 21, 1880/59
Cabinet service 1y 6m 1d

Alexander, Joshua W.   **CM**
Date of birth ....   Jan 22, 1852
Date of appointment/age ....   Dec 11, 1919/67
Assumed office/age ....   Dec 16, 1919/67
Left office/age ....   Mar 4, 1921/69
Date of death/age ....   Feb 27, 1936/84
Cabinet service 1y 2m 16d

Alger, Russell A.   **WR**
Date of birth ....   Feb 27, 1836
Date of appointment/age ....   Mar 5, 1897/61
Assumed office/age ....   Mar 5, 1897/61
Left office/age ....   Jul 31, 1899/63
Date of death/age ....   Jan 24, 1907/70
Cabinet service 2y 4m 26d

Anderson, Clinton P.   **AG**
Date of birth ....   Oct 23, 1895
Date of appointment/age ....   Jun 2, 1945/49
Assumed office/age ....   Jun 30, 1945/49
Left office/age ....   Jun 1, 1948/52
Date of death/age ....   Nov 11, 1975/80
Cabinet service 2y 11m 1d

Anderson, Robert B.   **TY**
Date of birth ....   Jun 4, 1910
Date of appointment/age ....   May 29, 1957/46
Assumed office/age ....   Jul 29, 1957/47
Left office/age ....   Jan 20, 1961/50
Date of death/age ....   — — —
Cabinet service 3y 5m 22d

Andrus, Cecil D.   **IN**
Date of birth ....   Aug 25, 1931
Date of appointment/age ....   Dec 19, 1976/45
Assumed office/age ....   Jan 21, 1977/45
Left office/age ....   Jan 20, 1981/49
Date of death/age ....   — — —
Cabinet service 4y

Armstrong, John   **WR**
Date of birth ....   Nov 25, 1758
Date of appointment/age ....   Jan 13, 1813/54
Assumed office/age ....   Feb 5, 1813/54
Left office/age ....   Aug 29, 1814/55
Date of death/age ....   Apr 1, 1843/84
Cabinet service 1y 6m 24d

Bacon, Robert   **ST**
Date of birth ....   Jul 5, 1860
Date of appointment/age ....   Jan 27, 1909/48
Assumed office/age ....   Jan 27, 1909/48
Left office/age ....   Mar 4, 1909/48
Date of death/age ....   May 29, 1919/58
Cabinet service 1m 5d

Badger, George E.   **NV**
Date of birth ....   Apr 17, 1795
Date of appointment/age ....   Mar 5, 1841/45
Assumed office/age ....   Mar 5, 1841/45
Left office/age ....   Sep 10, 1841/46
Date of death/age ....   May 11, 1866/71
Cabinet service 6m 5d

Baker, James A., III   **TY**
Date of birth ....   Apr 28, 1930
Date of appointment/age ....   Jan 10, 1985/54
Assumed office/age ....   Jan 29, 1985/54
Left office/age ....   — — —
Date of death/age ....   — — —
Cabinet service ....   — — —

Baker, Newton D.   **WR**
Date of birth ....   Dec 3, 1871
Date of appointment/age ....   Mar 7, 1916/44
Assumed office/age ....   Mar 9, 1916/44
Left office/age ....   Mar 4, 1921/49
Date of death/age ....   Dec 25, 1937/66
Cabinet service 4y 11m 26d

Baldridge, Malcolm   **CM**
Date of birth . . . . Oct 4, 1922
Date of appointment/age . . . . Dec 12, 1980/58
Assumed office/age . . . . Jan 23, 1981/58
Left office/age . . . . — — —
Date of death/age . . . . — — —
Cabinet service . . . . — — —

Ballinger, Richard A.   **IN**
Date of birth . . . . Jul 9, 1858
Date of appointment/age . . . . Mar 5, 1909/50
Assumed office/age . . . . Mar 5, 1909/50
Left office/age . . . . Mar 6, 1911/52
Date of death/age . . . . Jun 6, 1922/63
Cabinet service 2y 1d

Bancroft, George   **NV**
Date of birth . . . . Oct 3, 1800
Date of appointment/age . . . . Mar 10, 1845/44
Assumed office/age . . . . Mar 10, 1845/44
Left office/age . . . . Sep 8, 1846/45
Date of death/age . . . . Jan 17, 1891/90
Cabinet service 1y 5m 29d

Barbour, James   **WR**
Date of birth . . . . Jun 10, 1775
Date of appointment/age . . . . Mar 7, 1825/49
Assumed office/age . . . . Mar 7, 1825/49
Left office/age . . . . May 25, 1828/52
Date of death/age . . . . Jun 7, 1842/66
Cabinet service 3y 2m 18d

Barr, Joseph W.   **TY**
Date of birth . . . . Jan 17, 1918
Date of appointment/age . . . . Dec 24, 1968/50
Assumed office/age . . . . Dec 24, 1968/50
Left office/age . . . . Jan 20, 1969/50
Date of death/age . . . . — — —
Cabinet service 26d

Barry, William T.   **PG**
Date of birth . . . . Feb 5, 1785
Date of appointment/age . . . . Mar 9, 1829/44
Assumed office/age . . . . Apr 6, 1829/44
Left office/age . . . . Apr 30, 1835/50
Date of death/age . . . . Aug 30, 1835/50
Cabinet service 6y 24d

Bates, Edward   **AT**
Date of birth . . . . Sep 4, 1793
Date of appointment/age . . . . Mar 5, 1861/67
Assumed office/age . . . . Mar 5, 1861/67
Left office/age . . . . Dec 4, 1864/71
Date of death/age . . . . Mar 25, 1869/75
Cabinet service 3y 8m 29d

Bayard, Thomas F.   **ST**
Date of birth . . . . Oct 29, 1828
Date of appointment/age . . . . Mar 6, 1885/56
Assumed office/age . . . . Mar 6, 1885/56
Left office/age . . . . Mar 6, 1889/60
Date of death/age . . . . Sep 28, 1898/69
Cabinet service 4y

Belknap, William W.   **WR**
Date of birth . . . . Sep 22, 1829
Date of appointment/age . . . . Oct 25, 1869/40
Assumed office/age . . . . Nov 1, 1869/40
Left office/age . . . . Mar 1, 1876/46
Date of death/age . . . . Oct 13, 1890/61
Cabinet service 6y 4m

Bell, Griffin B.   **AT**
Date of birth . . . . Oct 31, 1918
Date of appointment/age . . . . Dec 21, 1976/58
Assumed office/age . . . . Jan 25, 1977/58
Left office/age . . . . Jul 20, 1979/60
Date of death/age . . . . — — —
Cabinet service 2y 5m 25d

Bell, John   **WR**
Date of birth .... Feb 15, 1797
Date of appointment/age .... Mar 5, 1841/44
Assumed office/age .... Mar 5, 1841/44
Left office/age .... Sep 11, 1841/44
Date of death/age .... Sep 10, 1869/72
Cabinet service 6m 6d

Bell, Terrel H.   **ED**
Date of birth .... Nov 11, 1921
Date of appointment/age .... Jan 8, 1981/59
Assumed office/age .... Jan 23, 1981/59
Left office/age .... Feb 7, 1985/64
Date of death/age .... — — —
Cabinet service 4y 15d

Bennett, William J.   **ED**
Date of birth .... Jul 31, 1943
Date of appointment/age .... Jan 10, 1985/41
Assumed office/age .... Feb 7, 1985/41
Left office/age .... — — —
Date of death/age .... — — —
Cabinet service .... — — —

Benson, Ezra T.   **AG**
Date of birth .... Aug 4, 1899
Date of appointment/age .... Jun 21, 1953/53
Assumed office/age .... Jun 21, 1953/53
Left office/age .... Jan 20, 1961/61
Date of death/age .... — — —
Cabinet service 7y 7m

Bergland, Robert S.   **AG**
Date of birth .... Jul 22, 1928
Date of appointment/age .... Dec 21, 1976/48
Assumed office/age .... Jan 21, 1977/48
Left office/age .... Jan 20, 1981/52
Date of death/age .... — — —
Cabinet service 4y

Berrien, John M.   **AT**
Date of birth .... Aug 23, 1781
Date of appointment/age .... Mar 9, 1829/47
Assumed office/age .... Mar 9, 1829/47
Left office/age .... Jun 22, 1831/49
Date of death/age .... Jan 1, 1856/74
Cabinet service 2y 3m 13d

Bibb, George M.   **TY**
Date of birth ....   Oct 30, 1776
Date of appointment/age ....   Jun 15, 1844/67
Assumed office/age ....   Jul 4, 1844/67
Left office/age ....   Mar 7, 1845/68
Date of death/age ....   Apr 14, 1859/82
Cabinet service 8m 3d

Biddle, Francis   **AT**
Date of birth ....   May 9, 1886
Date of appointment/age ....   Sep 5, 1941/55
Assumed office/age ....   Sep 5, 1941/55
Left office/age ....   Jun 30, 1945/59
Date of death/age ....   Oct 4, 1968/82
Cabinet service 3y 9m 25d

Bissell, Wilson S.   **PG**
Date of birth ....   Dec 31, 1847
Date of appointment/age ....   Mar 6, 1893/45
Assumed office/age ....   Mar 6, 1893/45
Left office/age ....   Apr 3, 1895/47
Date of death/age ....   Oct 6, 1903/55
Cabinet service 2y 28d

Black, Jeremiah S.   **AT**
Date of birth ....   Jan 10, 1810
Date of appointment/age ....   Mar 6, 1857/47
Assumed office/age ....   Mar 11, 1857/47
Left office/age ....   Dec 21, 1860/50
Date of death/age ....   Aug 19, 1883/73
Cabinet service 3y 9m 10d

Black, Jeremiah S.   **ST**
Date of birth ....   Jan 10, 1810
Date of appointment/age ....   Dec 17, 1860/50
Assumed office/age ....   Dec 17, 1860/50
Left office/age ....   Mar 4, 1861/51
Date of death/age ....   Aug 19, 1883/73
Cabinet service 2m 15d

Blaine, James G.　　　　　**ST**
Date of birth .... Jan 31, 1830
Date of appointment/age .... Mar 5, 1881/51
Assumed office/age .... Mar 7, 1881/51
Left office/age .... Dec 11, 1881/51
Date of death/age .... Jan 27, 1893/62
Cabinet service 9m 4d

Blaine, James G.　　　　　**ST**
Date of birth .... Jan 31, 1830
Date of appointment/age .... Mar 5, 1889/59
Assumed office/age .... Mar 7, 1889/59
Left office/age .... Jun 3, 1892/62
Date of death/age .... Jan 27, 1893/62
Cabinet service 3y 2m 26d

Blair, Montgomery　　　　　**PG**
Date of birth .... May 10, 1813
Date of appointment/age .... Mar 5, 1861/47
Assumed office/age .... Mar 9, 1861/47
Left office/age .... Sep 30, 1864/51
Date of death/age .... Jul 27, 1883/70
Cabinet service 3y 6m 21d

Bliss, Cornelius N.　　　　　**IN**
Date of birth .... Jan 26, 1883
Date of appointment/age .... Mar 5, 1897/64
Assumed office/age .... Mar 5, 1897/64
Left office/age .... Feb 19, 1899/66
Date of death/age .... Oct 9, 1911/78
Cabinet service 1y 11m 14d

Block, John R.　　　　　**AG**
Date of birth .... Feb 15, 1935
Date of appointment/age .... Dec 23, 1980/45
Assumed office/age .... Jan 20, 1981/45
Left office/age .... — — —
Date of death/age .... — — —
Cabinet service .... — — —

Blount, Winton M.   **PG**
Date of birth . . . .   Feb 1, 1921
Date of appointment/age . . . .   Jan 20, 1969/47
Assumed office/age . . . .   Jan 21, 1969/47
Left office/age . . . .   Jun 30, 1970/50
Date of death/age . . . .   — — —
Cabinet service 1y 5m 9d

Blumenthal, W. Michael   **TY**
Date of birth . . . .   Jan 3, 1926
Date of appointment/age . . . .   Dec 15, 1976/50
Assumed office/age . . . .   Jan 21, 1977/51
Left office/age . . . .   Jul 20, 1979/53
Date of death/age . . . .   — — —
Cabinet service 2y 5m 29d

Bonaparte, Charles J.   **NV**
Date of birth . . . .   Jun 9, 1851
Date of appointment/age . . . .   Jul 1, 1905/54
Assumed office/age . . . .   Jul 1, 1905/54
Left office/age . . . .   Dec 16, 1906/55
Date of death/age . . . .   Jun 28, 1921/70
Cabinet service 1y 5m 15d

Bonaparte, Charles J.   **AT**
Date of birth . . . .   Jun 9, 1851
Date of appointment/age . . . .   Dec 12, 1906/55
Assumed office/age . . . .   Dec 17, 1906/55
Left office/age . . . .   Mar 4, 1909/57
Date of death/age . . . .   Jun 28, 1921/70
Cabinet service 2y 2m 15d

Borie, Adolph E.   **NV**
Date of birth . . . .   Nov 25, 1809
Date of appointment/age . . . . . . — . .   Mar 5, 1869/59
Assumed office/age . . . .   Mar 9, 1869/59
Left office/age . . . .   Jun 24, 1869/59
Date of death/age . . . .   Feb 5, 1880/70
Cabinet service 3m 15d

Boutwell, George S.　　　　　　　**TY**
Date of birth . . . .　Jan 28, 1818
Date of appointment/age . . . .　Mar 11, 1869/51
Assumed office/age . . . .　Mar 11, 1869/51
Left office/age . . . .　Mar 16, 1873/55
Date of death/age . . . .　Feb 27, 1905/87
Cabinet service . . . .　4y 5d

Boyd, Alan S.　　　　　　　　　　**TR**
Date of birth . . . .　Jul 20, 1922
Date of appointment/age . . . .　Jan 10, 1967/46
Assumed office/age . . . .　Jan 16, 1967/46
Left office/age . . . .　Jan 20, 1969/47
Date of death/age . . . .　– – –
Cabinet service . . . .　2y 4d

Bradford, William　　　　　　　　**AT**
Date of birth . . . .　Sep 14, 1755
Date of appointment/age . . . .　Jan 28, 1794/38
Assumed office/age . . . .　Jan 29, 1794/38
Left office/age . . . .　Aug 23, 1795/39
Date of death/age . . . .　Aug 23, 1795/39
Cabinet service . . . .　1y 6m 25d

Branch, John　　　　　　　　　　**NV**
Date of birth . . . .　Nov 4, 1782
Date of appointment/age . . . .　Mar 9, 1829/46
Assumed office/age . . . .　Mar 9, 1829/46
Left office/age . . . .　May 11, 1831/48
Date of death/age . . . .　Jan 4, 1863/80
Cabinet service . . . .　2y 2m 2d

Brannan, Charles F.　　　　　　　**AG**
Date of birth . . . .　Aug 23, 1903
Date of appointment/age . . . .　May 29, 1948/44
Assumed office/age . . . .　Jun 2, 1948/44
Left office/age . . . .　Jan 20, 1953/49
Date of death/age . . . .　– – –
Cabinet service . . . .　4y 7m 18d

Breckenridge, John   **AT**
Date of birth ....   Dec 2, 1760
Date of appointment/age ....   Aug 7, 1805/44
Assumed office/age ....   Aug 7, 1805/44
Left office/age ....   Dec 14, 1806/46
Date of death/age ....   Dec 14, 1806/46
Cabinet service 1y 4m 7d

Brennan, Peter J.   **LB**
Date of birth ....   May 24, 1918
Date of appointment/age ....   Nov 29, 1972/54
Assumed office/age ....   Jan 31, 1973/54
Left office/age ....   Mar 1, 1975/56
Date of death/age ....   — — —
Cabinet service 2y 29d

Brewster, Benjamin H.   **AT**
Date of birth ....   Oct 13, 1816
Date of appointment/age ....   Dec 19, 1881/65
Assumed office/age ....   Jan 3, 1882/65
Left office/age ....   Mar 8, 1885/68
Date of death/age ....   Apr 4, 1888/71
Cabinet service 3y 2m 5d

Brinegar, Claude S.   **TR**
Date of birth ....   Dec 16, 1926
Date of appointment/age ....   Dec 7, 1972/45
Assumed office/age ....   Jan 19, 1973/46
Left office/age ....   Feb 1, 1975/47
Date of death/age ....   — — —
Cabinet service 2y 13d

Bristow, Benjamin H.   **TY**
Date of birth ....   Jun 20, 1832
Date of appointment/age ....   Jul 3, 1874/42
Assumed office/age ....   Jul 3, 1874/42
Left office/age ....   Jun 20, 1876/44
Date of death/age ....   Jun 22, 1890/58
Cabinet service 1y 11m 17d

Brown, Aaron V.   **PG**
Date of birth . . . .   Aug 15, 1795
Date of appointment/age . . . .   Mar 6, 1857/61
Assumed office/age . . . .   Mar 6, 1857/61
Left office/age . . . .   Mar 8, 1859/63
Date of death/age . . . .   Mar 8, 1859/63
Cabinet service 2y 2d

Brown, Harold   **DF**
Date of birth . . . .   Sep 19, 1927
Date of appointment/age . . . .   Dec 22, 1976/49
Assumed office/age . . . .   Jan 21, 1977/49
Left office/age . . . .   Jan 20, 1981/53
Date of death/age . . . .   − − −
Cabinet service 4y

Brown, Walter F.   **PG**
Date of birth . . . .   May 31, 1869
Date of appointment/age . . . .   Mar 5, 1929/59
Assumed office/age . . . .   Mar 6, 1929/59
Left office/age . . . .   Mar 3, 1933/63
Date of death/age . . . .   Jan 26, 1961/91
Cabinet service 3y 11m 27d

Brownell, Herbert, Jr.   **AT**
Date of birth . . . .   Feb 20, 1904
Date of appointment/age . . . .   Jan 21, 1953/48
Assumed office/age . . . .   Jan 21, 1953/48
Left office/age . . . .   Jan 26, 1958/53
Date of death/age . . . .   − − −
Cabinet service 5y 5d

Browning, Orville H.   **IN**
Date of birth . . . .   Feb 10, 1806
Date of appointment/age . . . .   Jul 27, 1866/60
Assumed office/age . . . .   Sep 1, 1866/60
Left office/age . . . .   Mar 3, 1869/63
Date of death/age . . . .   Aug 10, 1881/75
Cabinet service 2y 6m 2d

Bryan, William J. **ST**

Date of birth	Mar 18, 1860
Date of appointment/age	Mar 5, 1913/52
Assumed office/age	Mar 5, 1913/52
Left office/age	Jun 8, 1915/55
Date of death/age	Jul 26, 1925/65
Cabinet service	2y 3m 3d

Buchanan, James **ST**

Date of birth	Apr 23, 1791
Date of appointment/age	Mar 6, 1845/53
Assumed office/age	Mar 10, 1845/53
Left office/age	Mar 6, 1849/57
Date of death/age	Jun 1, 1868/77
Cabinet service	3y 11m 24d

Burleson, Albert S. **PG**

Date of birth	Jun 7, 1863
Date of appointment/age	Mar 5, 1913/49
Assumed office/age	Mar 5, 1913/49
Left office/age	Mar 4, 1921/57
Date of death/age	Nov 24, 1937/74
Cabinet service	8y

Butler, Benjamin F. **AT**

Date of birth	Dec 14, 1795
Date of appointment/age	Nov 15, 1833/37
Assumed office/age	Nov 18, 1833/37
Left office/age	Aug 31, 1838/42
Date of death/age	Nov 8, 1858/62
Cabinet service	4y 9m 13d

Butz, Earl L. **AG**

Date of birth	Jul 3, 1909
Date of appointment/age	Nov 11, 1971/62
Assumed office/age	Dec 2, 1971/62
Left office/age	Oct 5, 1976/67
Date of death/age	— — —
Cabinet service	4y 10m 3d

Byrnes, James F.   **ST**
Date of birth ....   May 2, 1879
Date of appointment/age ....   Jul 2, 1945/66
Assumed office/age ....   Jul 3, 1945/66
Left office/age ....   Jan 20, 1947/67
Date of death/age ....   Apr 9, 1972/92
Cabinet service 1y 6m 17d

Calhoun, John C.   **WR**
Date of birth ....   Mar 18, 1782
Date of appointment/age ....   Oct 8, 1817/35
Assumed office/age ....   Dec 10, 1817/35
Left office/age ....   Mar 3, 1825/42
Date of death/age ....   Mar 31, 1850/68
Cabinet service 7y 2m 21d

Calhoun, John C.   **ST**
Date of birth ....   Mar 18, 1782
Date of appointment/age ....   Mar 6, 1844/61
Assumed office/age ....   Apr 1, 1844/62
Left office/age ....   Mar 9, 1845/62
Date of death/age ....   Mar 31, 1850/68
Cabinet service 11m 8d

Califano, Joseph A., Jr.   **HW**
Date of birth ....   May 15, 1931
Date of appointment/age ....   Dec 24, 1976/45
Assumed office/age ....   Jan 25, 1977/45
Left office/age ....   Aug 4, 1979/48
Date of death/age ....   — — —
Cabinet service 2y 6m 10d

Cameron, James D.   **WR**
Date of birth ....   May 14, 1833
Date of appointment/age ....   May 22, 1876/43
Assumed office/age ....   Jun 1, 1876/43
Left office/age ....   Mar 11, 1877/43
Date of death/age ....   Aug 30, 1918/85
Cabinet service 9m 10d

Cameron, Simon — WR

Date of birth	Mar 8, 1799
Date of appointment/age	Mar 5, 1861/61
Assumed office/age	Mar 11, 1861/62
Left office/age	Jan 19, 1862/62
Date of death/age	Jun 26, 1889/90
Cabinet service	10m 8d

Campbell, George W. — TY

Date of birth	Feb 8, 1769
Date of appointment/age	Feb 9, 1814/45
Assumed office/age	Feb 9, 1814/45
Left office/age	Oct 13, 1814/45
Date of death/age	Feb 17, 1848/79
Cabinet service	8m 4d

Campbell, James — PG

Date of birth	Sep 1, 1812
Date of appointment/age	Mar 7, 1853/40
Assumed office/age	Mar 7, 1853/40
Left office/age	Mar 5, 1857/44
Date of death/age	Jan 27, 1893/80
Cabinet service	3y 11m 29d

Carlisle, John G. — TY

Date of birth	Sep 5, 1835
Date of appointment/age	Mar 6, 1893/57
Assumed office/age	Mar 6, 1893/57
Left office/age	Mar 4, 1897/61
Date of death/age	Jul 31, 1910/74
Cabinet service	3y 11m 28d

Cass, Lewis — WR

Date of birth	Oct 9, 1782
Date of appointment/age	Aug 1, 1831/48
Assumed office/age	Aug 8, 1831/48
Left office/age	Oct 4, 1836/53
Date of death/age	Jun 17, 1866/83
Cabinet service	5y 1m 26d

Cass, Lewis   **ST**
Date of birth .... Oct 9, 1782
Date of appointment/age .... Mar 6, 1857/74
Assumed office/age .... Mar 6, 1857/74
Left office/age .... Dec 14, 1860/78
Date of death/age .... Jun 17, 1866/83
Cabinet service 3y 9m 8d

Celebrezze, Anthony J.   **HW**
Date of birth .... Sep 4, 1910
Date of appointment/age .... Jul 31, 1962/51
Assumed office/age .... Jul 31, 1962/51
Left office/age .... Aug 17, 1965/54
Date of death/age .... — — —
Cabinet service 3y 17d

Chandler, William E.   **NV**
Date of birth .... Dec 28, 1835
Date of appointment/age .... Apr 12, 1882/46
Assumed office/age .... Apr 17, 1882/46
Left office/age .... Mar 5, 1885/49
Date of death/age .... Nov 30, 1917/81
Cabinet service 2y 10m 16d

Chandler, Zachariah   **IN**
Date of birth .... Dec 10, 1813
Date of appointment/age .... Oct 19, 1875/61
Assumed office/age .... Oct 19, 1875/61
Left office/age .... Mar 11, 1877/63
Date of death/age .... Nov 1, 1879/65
Cabinet service 1y 4m 20d

Chapin, Roy D.   **CM**
Date of birth .... Feb 23, 1880
Date of appointment/age .... Dec 14, 1932/52
Assumed office/age .... Dec 14, 1932/52
Left office/age .... Mar 3, 1933/53
Date of death/age .... Feb 16, 1936/55
Cabinet service 2m 17d

Chapman, Oscar L.				**IN**
Date of birth	Oct 22, 1896
Date of appointment/age	Nov 10, 1949/53
Assumed office/age	Jan 18, 1950/53
Left office/age	Jan 20, 1953/56
Date of death/age	Feb 8, 1978/81
Cabinet service	3y 2d

Chase, Salmon P.				**TY**
Date of birth	Jan 13, 1808
Date of appointment/age	Mar 5, 1861/53
Assumed office/age	Mar 7, 1861/53
Left office/age	Jul 4, 1864/56
Date of death/age	May 7, 1873/65
Cabinet service	3y 2m 27d

Civiletti, Benjamin R.				**AT**
Date of birth	Jul 17, 1935
Date of appointment/age	Jul 20, 1979/44
Assumed office/age	Aug 2, 1979/44
Left office/age	Jan 20, 1981/45
Date of death/age	— — —
Cabinet service	1y 5m 18d

Clark, Thomas C.				**AT**
Date of birth	Sep 23, 1899
Date of appointment/age	Jun 15, 1945/45
Assumed office/age	Jul 1, 1945/45
Left office/age	Aug 23, 1949/49
Date of death/age	Jun 13, 1977/78
Cabinet service	4y 1m 22d

Clark, William P.				**IN**
Date of birth	Oct 23, 1931
Date of appointment/age	Oct 13, 1983/51
Assumed office/age	Nov 19, 1983/52
Left office/age	Feb 7, 1985/53
Date of death/age	— — —
Cabinet service	1y 2m 19d

Clark, William Ramsey   **AT**
Date of birth . . . .   Dec 18, 1927
Date of appointment/age . . . .   Feb 28, 1967/39
Assumed office/age . . . .   Mar 10, 1967/39
Left office/age . . . .   Jan 20, 1969/41
Date of death/age . . . .   — — —
Cabinet service 1y 10m 10d

Clay, Henry   **ST**
Date of birth . . . .   Apr 12, 1777
Date of appointment/age . . . .   Mar 7, 1825/47
Assumed office/age . . . .   Mar 7, 1825/47
Left office/age . . . .   Mar 3, 1829/51
Date of death/age . . . .   Jun 29, 1852/75
Cabinet service 3y 11m 24d

Clayton, John M.   **ST**
Date of birth . . . .   Jul 24, 1796
Date of appointment/age . . . .   Mar 7, 1849/52
Assumed office/age . . . .   Mar 7, 1849/52
Left office/age . . . .   Jul 21, 1850/53
Date of death/age . . . .   Nov 9, 1856/60
Cabinet service 1y 4m 14d

Clifford, Clark M.   **DF**
Date of birth . . . .   Dec 25, 1906
Date of appointment/age . . . .   Jan 19, 1968/61
Assumed office/age . . . .   Mar 1, 1968/61
Left office/age . . . .   Jan 20, 1969/62
Date of death/age . . . .   — — —
Cabinet service 10m 19d

Clifford, Nathan   **AT**
Date of birth . . . .   Aug 18, 1803
Date of appointment/age . . . .   Oct 17, 1846/43
Assumed office/age . . . .   Oct 17, 1846/43
Left office/age . . . .   Mar 18, 1848/44
Date of death/age . . . .   Jul 25, 1881/77
Cabinet service 1y 5m 1d

Cobb, Howell   **TY**
Date of birth .... Sep 7, 1815
Date of appointment/age .... Mar 6, 1857/41
Assumed office/age .... Mar 6, 1857/41
Left office/age .... Dec 9, 1860/45
Date of death/age .... Oct 9, 1868/53
Cabinet service 3y 9m 3d

Cohen, Wilbur J.   **HW**
Date of birth .... Jun 10, 1913
Date of appointment/age .... Mar 23, 1968/55
Assumed office/age .... May 4, 1968/55
Left office/age .... Jan 20, 1969/55
Date of death/age .... — — —
Cabinet service 9m 28d

Colby, Bainbridge   **ST**
Date of birth .... Dec 22, 1869
Date of appointment/age .... Mar 22, 1920/50
Assumed office/age .... Mar 23, 1920/50
Left office/age .... Mar 3, 1921/51
Date of death/age .... Apr 11, 1950/80
Cabinet service 11m 20d

Coleman, William T., Jr.   **TR**
Date of birth .... Jul 7, 1920
Date of appointment/age .... Jan 15, 1975/54
Assumed office/age .... Mar 4, 1975/54
Left office/age .... Jan 20, 1977/56
Date of death/age .... — — —
Cabinet service 1y 10m 16d

Collamer, Jacob   **PG**
Date of birth .... Jan 8, 1791
Date of appointment/age ....—.. Mar 8, 1849/58
Assumed office/age .... Mar 8, 1849/58
Left office/age .... Jul 22, 1850/59
Date of death/age .... Nov 9, 1865/74
Cabinet service 1y 4m 14d

Colman, Norman J.   **AG**
Date of birth . . . .   May 16, 1827
Date of appointment/age . . . .   Feb 13, 1889/61
Assumed office/age . . . .   Feb 13, 1889/61
Left office/age . . . .   Mar 6, 1889/61
Date of death/age . . . .   Nov 3, 1911/84
Cabinet service 21d

Connally, John B.   **TY**
Date of birth . . . .   Feb 27, 1917
Date of appointment/age . . . .   Dec 14, 1970/53
Assumed office/age . . . .   Feb 11, 1971/53
Left office/age . . . .   May 16, 1972/54
Date of death/age . . . .   — — —
Cabinet service 1y 3m 5d

Connor, John T.   **CM**
Date of birth . . . .   Nov 3, 1914
Date of appointment/age . . . .   Jan 18, 1965/50
Assumed office/age . . . .   Jan 18, 1965/50
Left office/age . . . .   May 22, 1967/52
Date of death/age . . . .   — — —
Cabinet service 2y 4m 4d

Conrad, Charles M.   **WR**
Date of birth . . . .   Dec 24, 1804
Date of appointment/age . . . .   Aug 15, 1850/45
Assumed office/age . . . .   Aug 15, 1850/45
Left office/age . . . .   Mar 6, 1853/48
Date of death/age . . . .   Feb 11, 1878/73
Cabinet service 2y 6m 19d

Cortelyou, George B.   **CL**
Date of birth . . . .   Jul 26, 1862
Date of appointment/age . . . .   Feb 16, 1903/40
Assumed office/age . . . .   Feb 16, 1903/40
Left office/age . . . .   Jun 30, 1904/41
Date of death/age . . . .   Oct 23, 1940/78
Cabinet service 1y 4m 14d

Cortelyou, George B. **PG**
Date of birth .... Jul 26, 1862
Date of appointment/age .... Mar 6, 1905/42
Assumed office/age .... Mar 6, 1905/42
Left office/age .... Mar 3, 1907/44
Date of death/age .... Oct 23, 1940/78
Cabinet service 1y 11m 27d

Cortelyou, George B. **TY**
Date of birth .... Jul 26, 1862
Date of appointment/age .... Jan 15, 1907/44
Assumed office/age .... Mar 4, 1907/44
Left office/age .... Mar 7, 1909/46
Date of death/age .... Oct 23, 1940/78
Cabinet service 2y 3d

Corwin, Thomas **TY**
Date of birth .... Jul 29, 1794
Date of appointment/age .... Jul 23, 1850/55
Assumed office/age .... Jul 23, 1850/55
Left office/age .... Mar 6, 1853/58
Date of death/age .... Dec 18, 1865/71
Cabinet service 2y 7m 11d

Cox, Jacob D. **IN**
Date of birth .... Oct 27, 1828
Date of appointment/age .... Mar 5, 1869/40
Assumed office/age .... Mar 9, 1869/40
Left office/age .... Oct 31, 1870/42
Date of death/age .... Aug 8, 1900/71
Cabinet service 1y 7m 22d

Crawford, George W. **WR**
Date of birth .... Dec 22, 1798
Date of appointment/age .... Mar 8, 1849/50
Assumed office/age .... Mar 14, 1849/50
Left office/age .... Jul 22, 1850/51
Date of death/age .... Jul 22, 1872/73
Cabinet service 1y 4m 8d

Crawford, William H.   **WR**
Date of birth . . . .   Feb 24, 1772
Date of appointment/age . . . .   Aug 1, 1815/43
Assumed office/age . . . .   Aug 8, 1815/43
Left office/age . . . .   Oct 21, 1816/44
Date of death/age . . . .   Sep 15, 1834/62
Cabinet service 1y 2m 13d

Crawford, William H.   **TY**
Date of birth . . . .   Feb 24, 1772
Date of appointment/age . . . .   Oct 22, 1816/44
Assumed office/age . . . .   Oct 22, 1816/44
Left office/age . . . .   Mar 3, 1825/53
Date of death/age . . . .   Sep 15, 1834/62
Cabinet service 8y 4m 11d

Creswell, John A.J.   **PG**
Date of birth . . . .   Nov 18, 1828
Date of appointment/age . . . .   Mar 5, 1869/40
Assumed office/age . . . .   Mar 5, 1869/40
Left office/age . . . .   Jul 6, 1874/45
Date of death/age . . . .   Dec 23, 1891/63
Cabinet service 5y 4m 1d

Crittenden, John J.   **AT**
Date of birth . . . .   Sep 10, 1787
Date of appointment/age . . . .   Mar 5, 1841/53
Assumed office/age . . . .   Mar 5, 1841/53
Left office/age . . . .   Sep 11, 1841/54
Date of death/age . . . .   Jul 26, 1863/75
Cabinet service 6m 6d

Crittenden, John J.   **AT**
Date of birth . . . .   Sep 10, 1787
Date of appointment/age . . . .   Jul 22, 1850/62
Assumed office/age . . . .   Aug 14, 1850/62
Left office/age . . . .   Mar 6, 1853/65
Date of death/age . . . .   Jul 26, 1863/75
Cabinet service 2y 6m 20d

Crowninshield, Benjamin W.   NV
Date of birth . . . .   Dec 27, 1772
Date of appointment/age . . . .   Dec 19, 1814/41
Assumed office/age . . . .   Jan 16, 1815/42
Left office/age . . . .   Sep 30, 1818/45
Date of death/age . . . .   Feb 3, 1851/78
Cabinet service 3y 8m 14d

Cummings, Homer S.   AT
Date of birth . . . .   Apr 30, 1870
Date of appointment/age . . . .   Mar 4, 1933/62
Assumed office/age . . . .   Mar 4, 1933/62
Left office/age . . . .   Jan 1, 1939/68
Date of death/age . . . .   Sep 10, 1956/86
Cabinet service 5y 9m 28d

Cushing, Caleb   AT
Date of birth . . . .   Jan 17, 1800
Date of appointment/age . . . .   Mar 7, 1853/53
Assumed office/age . . . .   Mar 7, 1853/53
Left office/age . . . .   Mar 10, 1857/57
Date of death/age . . . .   Jan 2, 1879/78
Cabinet service 4y 3d

Dallas, Alexander J.   TY
Date of birth . . . .   Jun 21, 1759
Date of appointment/age . . . .   Oct 6, 1814/55
Assumed office/age . . . .   Oct 14, 1814/55
Left office/age . . . .   Oct 21, 1816/57
Date of death/age . . . .   Jan 16, 1817/57
Cabinet service 2y 7d

Daniels, Josephus   NV
Date of birth . . . .   May 18, 1862
Date of appointment/age . . . .   Mar 5, 1913/50
Assumed office/age . . . .   Mar 5, 1913/50
Left office/age . . . .   Mar 4, 1921/58
Date of death/age . . . .   Jan 15, 1948/85
Cabinet service 8y

Daugherty, Harry M.   **AT**

Date of birth	Jan 26, 1860
Date of appointment/age	Mar 5, 1921/61
Assumed office/age	Mar 5, 1921/61
Left office/age	Apr 8, 1924/64
Date of death/age	Oct 12, 1941/81
Cabinet service	3y 1m 3d

Davis, Dwight F.   **WR**

Date of birth	Jul 5, 1879
Date of appointment/age	Oct 13, 1925/46
Assumed office/age	Oct 14, 1925/46
Left office/age	Mar 5, 1929/49
Date of death/age	Nov 28, 1945/66
Cabinet service	3y 4m 19d

Davis, James J.   **LB**

Date of birth	Oct 27, 1873
Date of appointment/age	Mar 5, 1921/47
Assumed office/age	Mar 5, 1921/47
Left office/age	Dec 8, 1930/57
Date of death/age	Nov 22, 1947/74
Cabinet service	9y 9m 3d

Davis, Jefferson   **WR**

Date of birth	Jun 3, 1808
Date of appointment/age	Mar 7, 1853/44
Assumed office/age	Mar 7, 1853/44
Left office/age	Mar 2, 1857/48
Date of death/age	Dec 6, 1889/81
Cabinet service	3y 11m 25d

Day, J. Edward   **PG**

Date of birth	Oct 11, 1914
Date of appointment/age	Jan 21, 1961/46
Assumed office/age	Jan 21, 1961/46
Left office/age	Sep 29, 1963/48
Date of death/age	— — —
Cabinet service	2y 8m 8d

Day, William R.   **ST**
Date of birth .... Apr 17, 1849
Date of appointment/age .... Apr 26, 1898/49
Assumed office/age .... Apr 28, 1898/49
Left office/age .... Sep 16, 1898/49
Date of death/age .... Jul 9, 1923/74
Cabinet service 4m 19d

Dearborn, Henry   **WR**
Date of birth .... Feb 23, 1751
Date of appointment/age .... Mar 5, 1801/50
Assumed office/age .... Mar 5, 1801/50
Left office/age .... Feb 16, 1809/57
Date of death/age .... Jun 6, 1829/78
Cabinet service 7y 11m 11d

Delano, Columbus O.   **IN**
Date of birth .... Jun 5, 1809
Date of appointment/age .... Nov 1, 1870/61
Assumed office/age .... Nov 1, 1870/61
Left office/age .... Sep 30, 1875/65
Date of death/age .... Oct 23, 1896/87
Cabinet service 4y 10m 29d

Denby, Edwin   **NV**
Date of birth .... Feb 18, 1870
Date of appointment/age .... Mar 5, 1921/51
Assumed office/age .... Mar 5, 1921/51
Left office/age .... Mar 17, 1924/54
Date of death/age .... Feb 8, 1929/58
Cabinet service 3y 12d

Dennison, William   **PG**
Date of birth .... Nov 23, 1815
Date of appointment/age .... Sep 24, 1864/48
Assumed office/age .... Oct 1, 1864/48
Left office/age .... Jul 16, 1866/50
Date of death/age .... Jun 15, 1882/66
Cabinet service 1y 9m 15d

Dent, Frederick B.   **CM**
Date of birth .... Aug 17, 1922
Date of appointment/age .... Dec 6, 1972/50
Assumed office/age .... Jan 18, 1973/50
Left office/age .... Jan 20, 1975/52
Date of death/age .... — — —
Cabinet service 2y 2d

Dern, George H.   **WR**
Date of birth .... Sep 8, 1872
Date of appointment/age .... Mar 4, 1933/60
Assumed office/age .... Mar 4, 1933/60
Left office/age .... Aug 27, 1936/63
Date of death/age .... Aug 27, 1936/63
Cabinet service 3y 5m 23d

Devens, Charles   **AT**
Date of birth .... Apr 4, 1820
Date of appointment/age .... Mar 10, 1877/56
Assumed office/age .... Mar 12, 1877/56
Left office/age .... Mar 6, 1881/60
Date of death/age .... Jan 7, 1891/70
Cabinet service 3y 11m 24d

Dexter, Samuel   **WR**
Date of birth .... May 14, 1761
Date of appointment/age .... May 13, 1800/38
Assumed office/age .... Jun 12, 1800/39
Left office/age .... Dec 31, 1800/39
Date of death/age .... May 4, 1816/54
Cabinet service 6m 19d

Dexter, Samuel   **TY**
Date of birth .... May 14, 1761
Date of appointment/age .... Jan 1, 1801/39
Assumed office/age .... Jan 1, 1801/39
Left office/age .... May 6, 1801/39
Date of death/age .... May 4, 1816/54
Cabinet service 4m 5d

Dickerson, Mahlon NV
Date of birth . . . . Apr 17, 1770
Date of appointment/age . . . . Jun 30, 1834/64
Assumed office/age . . . . Jun 30, 1834/64
Left office/age . . . . Jun 30, 1838/68
Date of death/age . . . . Oct 5, 1853/83
Cabinet service 4y

Dickinson, Donald M. PG
Date of birth . . . . Jan 17, 1846
Date of appointment/age . . . . Jan 16, 1888/41
Assumed office/age . . . . Jan 16, 1888/41
Left office/age . . . . Mar 4, 1889/43
Date of death/age . . . . Oct 15, 1917/71
Cabinet service 1y 1m 16d

Dickinson, Jacob M. WR
Date of birth . . . . Jan 30, 1851
Date of appointment/age . . . . Mar 5, 1909/58
Assumed office/age . . . . Mar 12, 1909/58
Left office/age . . . . May 21, 1911/60
Date of death/age . . . . Dec 13, 1928/77
Cabinet service 2y 2m 9d

Dillon, C. Douglas TY
Date of birth . . . . Aug 21, 1909
Date of appointment/age . . . . Jan 21, 1961/51
Assumed office/age . . . . Jan 21, 1961/51
Left office/age . . . . Mar 31, 1965/55
Date of death/age . . . . — — —
Cabinet service 4y 2m 10d

Dix, John A. TY
Date of birth . . . . Jul 24, 1798
Date of appointment/age . . . . Jan 11, 1861/62
Assumed office/age . . . . Jan 15, 1861/62
Left office/age . . . . Mar 4, 1861/62
Date of death/age . . . . Apr 21, 1879/80
Cabinet service 1m 17d

Doak, William N.   **LB**
Date of birth .... Dec 12, 1882
Date of appointment/age .... Dec 8, 1930/47
Assumed office/age .... Dec 9, 1930/47
Left office/age .... Mar 3, 1933/50
Date of death/age .... Oct 23, 1933/50
Cabinet service 2y 2m 22d

Dobbin, James C.   **NV**
Date of birth .... Jan 17, 1814
Date of appointment/age .... Mar 7, 1853/39
Assumed office/age .... Mar 7, 1853/39
Left office/age .... Mar 5, 1857/43
Date of death/age .... Aug 4, 1857/43
Cabinet service 3y 11m 28d

Dole, Elizabeth H.   **TR**
Date of birth .... Jul 20, 1936
Date of appointment/age .... Jan 6, 1983/46
Assumed office/age .... Feb 8, 1983/46
Left office/age .... — — —
Date of death/age .... — — —
Cabinet service .... — — —

Donaldson, Jesse M.   **PG**
Date of birth .... Aug 17, 1885
Date of appointment/age .... Dec 16, 1947/62
Assumed office/age .... Dec 16, 1947/62
Left office/age .... Jan 20, 1953/67
Date of death/age .... Mar 25, 1970/84
Cabinet service 5y 1m 4d

Donovan, Raymond J.   **LB**
Date of birth .... Aug 31, 1930
Date of appointment/age .... Dec 17, 1980/50
Assumed office/age .... Jan 28, 1981/50
Left office/age .... — — —
Date of death/age .... — — —
Cabinet service .... — — —

Duane, William J.   **TY**
Date of birth ....   May 9, 1780
Date of appointment/age ....   May 29, 1833/53
Assumed office/age ....   Jun 1, 1833/53
Left office/age ....   Sep 22, 1833/53
Date of death/age ....   Sep 26, 1865/85
Cabinet service 3m 21d

Dulles, John Foster   **ST**
Date of birth ....   Feb 25, 1888
Date of appointment/age ....   Jan 21, 1953/64
Assumed office/age ....   Jan 21, 1953/64
Left office/age ....   Apr 21, 1959/71
Date of death/age ....   May 24, 1959/71
Cabinet service 6y 3m

Duncan, Charles W., Jr.   **EN**
Date of birth ....   Sep 9, 1926
Date of appointment/age ....   Jul 21, 1979/52
Assumed office/age ....   Jul 31, 1979/52
Left office/age ....   Jan 20, 1981/54
Date of death/age ....   — — —
Cabinet service 1y 5m 20d

Dunlop, John T.   **LB**
Date of birth ....   Jul 5, 1914
Date of appointment/age ....   Feb 9, 1975/60
Assumed office/age ....   Mar 7, 1975/60
Left office/age ....   Feb 1, 1976/61
Date of death/age ....   — — —
Cabinet service 10m 25d

Durkin, Martin P.   **LB**
Date of birth ....   Mar 18, 1894
Date of appointment/age ....   Jan 21, 1953/58
Assumed office/age ....   Jan 21, 1953/58
Left office/age ....   Oct 8, 1953/59
Date of death/age ....   Nov 13, 1955/61
Cabinet service 8m 17d

Eaton, John H.   **WR**
Date of birth ....   Jun 18, 1790
Date of appointment/age ....   Mar 9, 1829/38
Assumed office/age ....   Mar 9, 1829/38
Left office/age ....   Jun 19, 1831/41
Date of death/age ....   Nov 17, 1856/66
Cabinet service 2y 3m 10d

Edison, Charles   **NV**
Date of birth ....   Aug 3, 1890
Date of appointment/age ....   Jan 11, 1940/49
Assumed office/age ....   Jan 11, 1940/49
Left office/age ....   Jul 9, 1940/49
Date of death/age ....   Jul 31, 1969/78
Cabinet service 5m 28d

Edwards, James B.   **EN**
Date of birth ....   Jun 24, 1927
Date of appointment/age ....   Dec 23, 1980/53
Assumed office/age ....   Jan 23, 1981/53
Left office/age ....   Nov 5, 1982/55
Date of death/age ....   — — —
Cabinet service 1y 9m 13d

Elkins, Stephen B.   **WR**
Date of birth ....   Sep 26, 1841
Date of appointment/age ....   Dec 22, 1891/50
Assumed office/age ....   Dec 24, 1891/50
Left office/age ....   Mar 5, 1893/51
Date of death/age ....   Jan 4, 1911/69
Cabinet service 1y 2m 9d

Endicott, William C.   **WR**
Date of birth ....   Nov 19, 1826
Date of appointment/age ....   Mar 6, 1885/58
Assumed office/age ....   Mar 6, 1885/58
Left office/age ....   Mar 4, 1889/62
Date of death/age ....   May 6, 1900/73
Cabinet service 3y 11m 28d

Eustis, William   **WR**
Date of birth . . . .   Jun 10, 1753
Date of appointment/age . . . .   Mar 7, 1809/55
Assumed office/age . . . .   Apr 8, 1809/55
Left office/age . . . .   Dec 31, 1812/59
Date of death/age . . . .   Feb 6, 1825/71
Cabinet service 3y 8m 23d

Evarts, William M.   **AT**
Date of birth . . . .   Feb 6, 1818
Date of appointment/age . . . .   Jul 15, 1868/50
Assumed office/age . . . .   Jul 20, 1868/50
Left office/age . . . .   Mar 4, 1869/51
Date of death/age . . . .   Feb 28, 1901/83
Cabinet service 7m 12d

Evarts, William M.   **ST**
Date of birth . . . .   Feb 6, 1818
Date of appointment/age . . . .   Mar 12, 1877/59
Assumed office/age . . . .   Mar 12, 1877/59
Left office/age . . . .   Mar 6, 1881/63
Date of death/age . . . .   Feb 28, 1901/83
Cabinet service 3y 11m 22d

Everett, Edward   **ST**
Date of birth . . . .   Apr 11, 1794
Date of appointment/age . . . .   Nov 6, 1852/58
Assumed office/age . . . .   Nov 6, 1852/58
Left office/age . . . .   Mar 3, 1853/58
Date of death/age . . . .   Jan 15, 1865/70
Cabinet service 3m 25d

Ewing, Thomas   **TY**
Date of birth . . . .   Dec 28, 1789
Date of appointment/age . . . .   Mar 5, 1841/51
Assumed office/age . . . .   Mar 5, 1841/51
Left office/age . . . .   Sep 12, 1841/51
Date of death/age . . . .   Oct 6, 1871/81
Cabinet service 6m 7d

Ewing, Thomas   **IN**
Date of birth .... Dec 28, 1789
Date of appointment/age .... Mar 8, 1849/59
Assumed office/age .... Mar 8, 1849/59
Left office/age .... Jul 22, 1850/60
Date of death/age .... Oct 26, 1871/81
Cabinet service 1y 4m 14d

Fairchild, Charles S.   **TY**
Date of birth .... Apr 30, 1842
Date of appointment/age .... Apr 1, 1887/44
Assumed office/age .... Apr 1, 1887/44
Left office/age .... Mar 6, 1889/46
Date of death/age .... Nov 24, 1924/82
Cabinet service 1y 11m 5d

Fall, Albert B.   **IN**
Date of birth .... Nov 26, 1861
Date of appointment/age .... Mar 5, 1921/59
Assumed office/age .... Mar 5, 1921/59
Left office/age .... Mar 4, 1923/61
Date of death/age .... Nov 30, 1944/83
Cabinet service 2y

Farley, James A.   **PG**
Date of birth .... May 30, 1888
Date of appointment/age .... Mar 4, 1933/44
Assumed office/age .... Mar 4, 1933/44
Left office/age .... Sep 9, 1940/52
Date of death/age .... Jun 9, 1976/88
Cabinet service 7y 6m 5d

Fessenden, William P.   **TY**
Date of birth .... Oct 16, 1806
Date of appointment/age .... Jul 1, 1864/57
Assumed office/age .... Jul 5, 1864/57
Left office/age .... Mar 3, 1865/58
Date of death/age .... Sep 8, 1869/62
Cabinet service 7m 26d

Finch, Robert H.   **HW**
Date of birth .... Oct 9, 1925
Date of appointment/age .... Jan 20, 1969/43
Assumed office/age .... Jan 22, 1969/43
Left office/age .... Jun 6, 1970/44
Date of death/age .... — — —
Cabinet service 1y 4m 15d

Fish, Hamilton   **ST**
Date of birth .... Aug 3, 1808
Date of appointment/age .... Mar 11, 1869/60
Assumed office/age .... Mar 17, 1869/60
Left office/age .... Mar 11, 1877/68
Date of death/age .... Sep 6, 1893/85
Cabinet service 7y 11m 22d

Fisher, Walter L.   **IN**
Date of birth .... Jul 4, 1862
Date of appointment/age .... Mar 7, 1911/48
Assumed office/age .... Mar 7, 1911/48
Left office/age .... Mar 4, 1913/50
Date of death/age .... Nov 9, 1935/73
Cabinet service 1y 11m 25d

Flemming, Arthur S.   **HW**
Date of birth .... Jun 12, 1905
Date of appointment/age .... Aug 1, 1958/53
Assumed office/age .... Aug 1, 1958/53
Left office/age .... Jan 20, 1961/55
Date of death/age .... — — —
Cabinet service 2y 5m 19d

Floyd, John B.   **WR**
Date of birth .... Jun 1, 1806
Date of appointment/age .... Mar 6, 1857/50
Assumed office/age .... Mar 6, 1857/50
Left office/age .... Jan 17, 1861/54
Date of death/age .... Aug 26, 1863/57
Cabinet service 3y 10m 11d

Folger, Charles J.   **TY**
Date of birth .... Apr 16, 1818
Date of appointment/age .... Oct 27, 1881/63
Assumed office/age .... Nov 14, 1881/63
Left office/age .... Sep 4, 1884/66
Date of death/age .... Sep 4, 1884/66
Cabinet service 2y 9m 21d

Folsom, Marion B.   **HW**
Date of birth .... Nov 23, 1893
Date of appointment/age .... Aug 1, 1955/61
Assumed office/age .... Aug 1, 1955/61
Left office/age .... Jul 31, 1958/64
Date of death/age .... Sep 28, 1976/82
Cabinet service 3y

Forrestal, James V.   **NV**
Date of birth .... Feb 15, 1892
Date of appointment/age .... May 18, 1944/52
Assumed office/age .... May 18, 1944/52
Left office/age .... Sep 17, 1947/55
Date of death/age .... May 22, 1949/57
Cabinet service 3y 4m

Forrestal, James V.   **DF**
Date of birth .... Feb 15, 1892
Date of appointment/age .... Aug 21, 1947/55
Assumed office/age .... Sep 17, 1947/55
Left office/age .... Mar 22, 1949/57
Date of death/age .... May 22, 1949/57
Cabinet service 1y 6m 5d

Forsyth, John   **ST**
Date of birth .... Oct 22, 1780
Date of appointment/age .... Jun 27, 1834/53
Assumed office/age .... Jul 1, 1834/53
Left office/age .... Mar 3, 1841/60
Date of death/age .... Oct 21, 1841/60
Cabinet service 6y 8m 2d

Forward, Walter   **TY**
Date of birth .... Jan 24, 1786
Date of appointment/age .... Sep 13, 1841/55
Assumed office/age .... Sep 13, 1841/55
Left office/age .... Feb 28, 1843/57
Date of death/age .... Nov 24, 1852/66
Cabinet service 1y 5m 15d

Foster, Charles   **TY**
Date of birth .... Apr 12, 1828
Date of appointment/age .... Feb 24, 1891/62
Assumed office/age .... Feb 24, 1891/62
Left office/age .... Mar 5, 1893/64
Date of death/age .... Jan 9, 1904/75
Cabinet service 2y 9d

Foster, John W.   **ST**
Date of birth .... Mar 2, 1836
Date of appointment/age .... Jun 29, 1892/56
Assumed office/age .... Jun 29, 1892/56
Left office/age .... Feb 22, 1893/56
Date of death/age .... Nov 15, 1917/81
Cabinet service 7m 24d

Fowler, Henry H.   **TY**
Date of birth .... Sep 5, 1908
Date of appointment/age .... Apr 1, 1965/56
Assumed office/age .... Apr 1, 1965/56
Left office/age .... Dec 20, 1968/60
Date of death/age .... — — —
Cabinet service 3y 8m 19d

Francis, David R.   **IN**
Date of birth .... Oct 1, 1850
Date of appointment/age .... Sep 1, 1896/45
Assumed office/age .... Sep 4, 1896/45
Left office/age .... Mar 4, 1897/46
Date of death/age .... Jan 15, 1927/76
Cabinet service 6m

Freeman, Orville L.   **AG**
Date of birth . . . .   May 9, 1918
Date of appointment/age . . . .   Jan 21, 1961/42
Assumed office/age . . . .   Jan 21, 1961/42
Left office/age . . . .   Jan 20, 1969/50
Date of death/age . . . .   — — —
Cabinet service 8y

Frelinghuysen, Frederick T.   **ST**
Date of birth . . . .   Aug 4, 1817
Date of appointment/age . . . .   Dec 12, 1881/64
Assumed office/age . . . .   Dec 19, 1881/64
Left office/age . . . .   Mar 5, 1885/67
Date of death/age . . . .   May 20, 1885/67
Cabinet service 3y 2m 14d

Gage, Lyman J.   **TY**
Date of birth . . . .   Jun 28, 1836
Date of appointment/age . . . .   Mar 5, 1897/60
Assumed office/age . . . .   Mar 5, 1897/60
Left office/age . . . .   Jan 30, 1902/65
Date of death/age . . . .   Jan 26, 1927/90
Cabinet service 4y 10m 25d

Gallatin, Albert   **TY**
Date of birth . . . .   Jan 29, 1761
Date of appointment/age . . . .   May 14, 1801/40
Assumed office/age . . . .   May 15, 1801/40
Left office/age . . . .   Feb 8, 1814/53
Date of death/age . . . .   Aug 12, 1849/88
Cabinet service 12y 8m 24d

Gardner, John W.   **HW**
Date of birth . . . .   Oct 8, 1912
Date of appointment/age . . . .   Jul 27, 1965/52
Assumed office/age . . . .   Aug 18, 1965/52
Left office/age . . . .   Mar 1, 1968/55
Date of death/age . . . .   — — —
Cabinet service 2y 6m 11d

Garfield, James R.   **IN**
Date of birth ....   Oct 17, 1865
Date of appointment/age ....   Jan 15, 1907/41
Assumed office/age ....   Mar 4, 1907/41
Left office/age ....   Mar 5, 1909/43
Date of death/age ....   Mar 24, 1950/84
Cabinet service 2y 1d

Garland, Augustus H.   **AT**
Date of birth ....   Jun 11, 1832
Date of appointment/age ....   Mar 6, 1885/52
Assumed office/age ....   Mar 9, 1885/52
Left office/age ....   Mar 4, 1889/56
Date of death/age ....   Jan 26, 1899/66
Cabinet service 3y 11m 26d

Garrison, Lindley M.   **WR**
Date of birth ....   Nov 28, 1864
Date of appointment/age ....   Mar 5, 1913/48
Assumed office/age ....   Mar 5, 1913/48
Left office/age ....   Feb 11, 1916/51
Date of death/age ....   Oct 19, 1932/67
Cabinet service 2y 11m 6d

Gary, James A.   **PG**
Date of birth ....   Oct 22, 1833
Date of appointment/age ....   Mar 5, 1897/63
Assumed office/age ....   Mar 5, 1897/63
Left office/age ....   Apr 20, 1898/64
Date of death/age ....   Oct 31, 1920/87
Cabinet service 1y 1m 15d

Gilmer, Thomas W.   **NV**
Date of birth ....   Apr 6, 1802
Date of appointment/age ....   Feb 15, 1844/41
Assumed office/age ....   Feb 19, 1844/41
Left office/age ....   Feb 28, 1844/41
Date of death/age ....   Feb 28, 1844/41
Cabinet service 9d

Gilpin, Henry D.   **AT**

Date of birth	Apr 14, 1801
Date of appointment/age	Jan 11, 1840/38
Assumed office/age	Jan 11, 1840/38
Left office/age	Mar 3, 1841/39
Date of death/age	Jan 29, 1860/58
Cabinet service	1y 1m 20d

Glass, Carter   **TY**

Date of birth	Jan 4, 1858
Date of appointment/age	Dec 6, 1918/60
Assumed office/age	Dec 16, 1918/60
Left office/age	Feb 1, 1920/62
Date of death/age	May 28, 1946/88
Cabinet service	1y 1m 16d

Goff, Nathan, Jr.   **NV**

Date of birth	Feb 9, 1843
Date of appointment/age	Jan 6, 1881/37
Assumed office/age	Jan 6, 1881/37
Left office/age	Mar 6, 1881/38
Date of death/age	Apr 24, 1920/77
Cabinet service	2m

Goldberg, Arthur J.   **LB**

Date of birth	Aug 8, 1908
Date of appointment/age	Jan 21, 1961/52
Assumed office/age	Jan 21, 1961/52
Left office/age	Sep 24, 1962/54
Date of death/age	— — —
Cabinet service	1y 8m 3d

Goldschmidt, Neil E.   **TR**

Date of birth	Jun 16, 1940
Date of appointment/age	Jul 28, 1979/39
Assumed office/age	Sep 22, 1979/39
Left office/age	Jan 20, 1981/40
Date of death/age	— — —
Cabinet service	1y 3m 28d

Good, James W.   **WR**
Date of birth . . . .   Sep 24, 1866
Date of appointment/age . . . .   Mar 5, 1929/62
Assumed office/age . . . .   Mar 6, 1929/62
Left office/age . . . .   Nov 11, 1929/63
Date of death/age . . . .   Nov 11, 1929/63
Cabinet service 8m 3d

Gore, Howard M.   **AG**
Date of birth . . . .   Oct 12, 1887
Date of appointment/age . . . .   Nov 21, 1924/37
Assumed office/age . . . .   Nov 22, 1924/37
Left office/age . . . .   Mar 4, 1925/37
Date of death/age . . . .   Jun 20, 1947/60
Cabinet service 3m 10d

Graham, William A.   **NV**
Date of birth . . . .   Sep 5, 1804
Date of appointment/age . . . .   Jul 22, 1850/45
Assumed office/age . . . .   Aug 2, 1850/45
Left office/age . . . .   Jul 25, 1852/47
Date of death/age . . . .   Aug 11, 1875/70
Cabinet service 1y 11m 23d

Granger, Francis   **PG**
Date of birth . . . .   Dec 1, 1792
Date of appointment/age . . . .   Mar 6, 1841/48
Assumed office/age . . . .   Mar 8, 1841/48
Left office/age . . . .   Sep 13, 1841/48
Date of death/age . . . .   Aug 28, 1868/75
Cabinet service 6m 5d

Granger, Gideon   **PG**
Date of birth . . . .   Jul 19, 1767
Date of appointment/age . . . .   Nov 28, 1801/34
Assumed office/age . . . .   Nov 28, 1801/34
Left office/age . . . .   Apr 10, 1814/46
Date of death/age . . . .   Dec 31, 1822/55
Cabinet service 12y 4m 13d

Gregory, Thomas W.   **AT**
Date of birth ....   Nov 6, 1861
Date of appointment/age ....   Aug 29, 1914/52
Assumed office/age ....   Sep 3, 1914/52
Left office/age ....   Mar 4, 1919/57
Date of death/age ....   Feb 26, 1933/71
Cabinet service 4y 6m 1d

Gresham, Walter Q.   **PG**
Date of birth ....   Mar 17, 1832
Date of appointment/age ....   Apr 3, 1883/51
Assumed office/age ....   Apr 11, 1883/51
Left office/age ....   Sep 24, 1884/52
Date of death/age ....   May 28, 1895/63
Cabinet service 1y 5m 13d

Gresham, Walter Q.   **TY**
Date of birth ....   Mar 17, 1832
Date of appointment/age ....   Sep 24, 1884/52
Assumed office/age ....   Sep 25, 1884/52
Left office/age ....   Oct 28, 1884/52
Date of death/age ....   May 28, 1895/63
Cabinet service 1m 3d

Gresham, Walter Q.   **ST**
Date of birth ....   Mar 17, 1832
Date of appointment/age ....   Mar 6, 1893/60
Assumed office/age ....   Mar 6, 1893/60
Left office/age ....   May 28, 1895/63
Date of death/age ....   May 28, 1895/63
Cabinet service 2y 2m 22d

Griggs, John W.   **AT**
Date of birth ....   Jul 10, 1849
Date of appointment/age ....   Jan 25, 1898/48
Assumed office/age ....   Feb 1, 1898/48
Left office/age ....   Mar 31, 1901/51
Date of death/age ....   Nov 28, 1927/78
Cabinet service 3y 2m

Gronouski, John A.   **PG**
Date of birth .... Oct 26, 1919
Date of appointment/age .... Sep 30, 1963/43
Assumed office/age .... Sep 30, 1963/43
Left office/age .... Nov 2, 1965/46
Date of death/age .... — — —
Cabinet service 2y 1m 3d

Grundy, Felix   **AT**
Date of birth .... Sep 11, 1777
Date of appointment/age .... Jul 5, 1838/60
Assumed office/age .... Sep 1, 1838/60
Left office/age .... Jan 10, 1840/62
Date of death/age .... Dec 19, 1840/63
Cabinet service 1y 4m 9d

Guthrie, James   **TY**
Date of birth .... Dec 5, 1792
Date of appointment/age .... Mar 7, 1853/60
Assumed office/age .... Mar 7, 1853/60
Left office/age .... Mar 5, 1857/64
Date of death/age .... Mar 13, 1869/76
Cabinet service 3y 11m 28d

Habersham, Joseph   **PG**
Date of birth .... Jul 28, 1751
Date of appointment/age .... Feb 25, 1795/43
Assumed office/age .... Feb 25, 1795/43
Left office/age .... Nov 27, 1801/50
Date of death/age .... Nov 17, 1815/64
Cabinet service 6y 9m 2d

Haig, Alexander M., Jr.   **ST**
Date of birth .... Dec 2, 1924
Date of appointment/age .... Dec 17, 1980/56
Assumed office/age .... Jan 22, 1981/56
Left office/age .... Jun 26, 1982/57
Date of death/age .... — — —
Cabinet service 1y 5m 4d

Hall, Nathan K.   **PG**
Date of birth .... Mar 28, 1810
Date of appointment/age .... Jul 23, 1850/40
Assumed office/age .... Jul 23, 1850/40
Left office/age .... Aug 31, 1852/42
Date of death/age .... Mar 2, 1874/63
Cabinet service 2y 1m 21d

Hamilton, Alexander   **TY**
Date of birth .... Jan 11, 1757
Date of appointment/age .... Sep 11, 1789/32
Assumed office/age .... Sep 11, 1789/32
Left office/age .... Feb 1, 1975/38
Date of death/age .... Jul 12, 1804/47
Cabinet service 5y 4m 21d

Hamilton, Paul   **NV**
Date of birth .... Oct 16, 1762
Date of appointment/age .... Mar 7, 1809/46
Assumed office/age .... May 15, 1809/46
Left office/age .... Dec 31, 1812/50
Date of death/age .... Jun 30, 1816/53
Cabinet service 3y 7m 16d

Hannegan, Robert E.   **PG**
Date of birth .... Jun 30, 1903
Date of appointment/age .... May 8, 1945/41
Assumed office/age .... Jul 1, 1945/42
Left office/age .... Dec 15, 1947/44
Date of death/age .... Oct 6, 1949/46
Cabinet service 2y 5m 14d

Hardin, Clifford   **AG**
Date of birth .... Oct 9, 1915
Date of appointment/age .... Jan 20, 1969/53
Assumed office/age .... Jan 22, 1969/53
Left office/age .... Nov 11, 1971/56
Date of death/age .... — — —
Cabinet service 2y 9m 19d

Harlan, James   **IN**

Date of birth	Aug 26, 1820
Date of appointment/age	May 15, 1865/44
Assumed office/age	May 15, 1865/44
Left office/age	Aug 31, 1866/46
Date of death/age	Oct 5, 1899/79
Cabinet service	1y 3m 16d

Harmon, Judson   **AT**

Date of birth	Feb 3, 1846
Date of appointment/age	Jun 8, 1895/49
Assumed office/age	Jun 11, 1895/49
Left office/age	Mar 6, 1897/51
Date of death/age	Feb 22, 1927/81
Cabinet service	1y 8m 23d

Harriman, William Averell   **CM**

Date of birth	Nov 15, 1891
Date of appointment/age	Jan 28, 1947/55
Assumed office/age	Jan 28, 1947/55
Left office/age	May 5, 1948/56
Date of death/age	— — —
Cabinet service	1y 3m 7d

Harris, Patricia R.   **HD**

Date of birth	May 31, 1924
Date of appointment/age	Dec 22, 1976/52
Assumed office/age	Jan 21, 1977/52
Left office/age	Aug 4, 1979/55
Date of death/age	— — —
Cabinet service	2y 6m 14d

Harris, Patricia R.   **HW**

Date of birth	May 31, 1924
Date of appointment/age	Jul 20, 1979/55
Assumed office/age	Aug 4, 1979/55
Left office/age	Oct 18, 1979/55
Date of death/age	— — —
Cabinet service	2m 14d

Harris, Patricia R.　　　　　　　**HH**
Date of birth .... May 31, 1924
Date of appointment/age .... Oct 18, 1979/55
Assumed office/age .... Oct 18, 1979/55
Left office/age .... Jan 20, 1981/56
Date of death/age .... — — —
Cabinet service 1y 3m 2d

Hathaway, Stanley K.　　　　　　**IN**
Date of birth .... Jul 19, 1924
Date of appointment/age .... Apr 4, 1975/50
Assumed office/age .... Jun 12, 1975/50
Left office/age .... Jul 25, 1975/51
Date of death/age .... — — —
Cabinet service 1m 13d

Hatton, Frank　　　　　　　　　**PG**
Date of birth .... Apr 28, 1846
Date of appointment/age .... Oct 14, 1884/38
Assumed office/age .... Oct 14, 1884/38
Left office/age .... Mar 5, 1885/38
Date of death/age .... Apr 30, 1894/48
Cabinet service 4m 19d

Hay, John　　　　　　　　　　　**ST**
Date of birth .... Oct 8, 1838
Date of appointment/age .... Sep 20, 1898/59
Assumed office/age .... Sep 30, 1898/59
Left office/age .... Jul 1, 1905/66
Date of death/age .... Jul 1, 1905/66
Cabinet service 6y 9m 1d

Hays, Will H.　　　　　　　　　**PG**
Date of birth .... Nov 5, 1879
Date of appointment/age .... Mar 5, 1921/41
Assumed office/age .... Mar 5, 1921/41
Left office/age .... Mar 3, 1922/42
Date of death/age .... Mar 7, 1954/74
Cabinet service 11m 28d

Heckler, Margaret M. HH
Date of birth . . . . Jun 21, 1931
Date of appointment/age . . . . Jan 12, 1983/51
Assumed office/age . . . . Mar 4, 1983/51
Left office/age . . . . — — —
Date of death/age . . . . — — —
Cabinet service . . . . — — —

Henshaw, David NV
Date of birth . . . . Apr 2, 1791
Date of appointment/age . . . . Jul 24, 1843/52
Assumed office/age . . . . Jul 24, 1843/52
Left office/age . . . . Feb 18, 1844/52
Date of death/age . . . . Nov 11, 1852/61
Cabinet service 6m 25d

Herbert, Hilary A. NV
Date of birth . . . . Mar 12, 1834
Date of appointment/age . . . . Mar 6, 1893/58
Assumed office/age . . . . Mar 6, 1893/58
Left office/age . . . . Mar 4, 1897/62
Date of death/age . . . . Mar 6, 1919/84
Cabinet service 3y 11m 28d

Herrington, John S. EN
Date of birth . . . . May 31, 1939
Date of appointment/age . . . . Jan 10, 1985/45
Assumed office/age . . . . Feb 7, 1985/45
Left office/age . . . . — — —
Date of death/age . . . . — — —
Cabinet service . . . . — — —

Herter, Christian A. ST
Date of birth . . . . Mar 28, 1895
Date of appointment/age . . . . Apr 22, 1959/64
Assumed office/age . . . . Apr 22, 1959/64
Left office/age . . . . Jan 20, 1961/65
Date of death/age . . . . Dec 30, 1967/72
Cabinet service 1y 8m 29d

Hickel, Walter J. IN
Date of birth . . . . Aug 18, 1919
Date of appointment/age . . . . Jan 20, 1969/49
Assumed office/age . . . . Jan 24, 1969/49
Left office/age . . . . Nov 25, 1970/51
Date of death/age . . . . — — —
Cabinet service 1y 10m 1d

Hills, Carla A.   **HD**
Date of birth .... Jan 3, 1934
Date of appointment/age .... Feb 14, 1975/41
Assumed office/age .... Mar 6, 1975/41
Left office/age .... Jan 20, 1977/43
Date of death/age .... — — —
Cabinet service 1y 10m 14d

Hitchcock, Ethan A.   **IN**
Date of birth .... Sep 19, 1835
Date of appointment/age .... Dec 21, 1898/63
Assumed office/age .... Feb 20, 1899/63
Left office/age .... Mar 3, 1907/71
Date of death/age .... Apr 9, 1909/73
Cabinet service 8y 11d

Hitchcock, Frank H.   **PG**
Date of birth .... Oct 5, 1869
Date of appointment/age .... Mar 5, 1909/39
Assumed office/age .... Mar 5, 1909/39
Left office/age .... Mar 4, 1913/43
Date of death/age .... Aug 5, 1935/65
Cabinet service 4y

Hoar, Ebenezer   **AT**
Date of birth .... Feb 21, 1816
Date of appointment/age .... Mar 5, 1869/53
Assumed office/age .... Mar 11, 1869/53
Left office/age .... Jul 7, 1870/54
Date of death/age .... Jan 31, 1895/79
Cabinet service 1y 3m 26d

Hobby, Oveta C.   **HW**
Date of birth .... Jan 19, 1905
Date of appointment/age .... Apr 11, 1953/48
Assumed office/age .... Apr 11, 1953/48
Left office/age .... Jul 31, 1955/50
Date of death/age .... — — —
Cabinet service 2y 3m 20d

Hodel, Donald P.   **EN**
Date of birth ....   May 23, 1935
Date of appointment/age ....   Nov 6, 1982/47
Assumed office/age ....   Dec 8, 1982/47
Left office/age ....   Feb 7, 1985/49
Date of death/age ....   — — —
Cabinet service 2y 2m

Hodel, Donald P.   **IN**
Date of birth ....   May 23, 1935
Date of appointment/age ....   Jan 10, 1985/49
Assumed office/age ....   Feb 7, 1985/49
Left office/age ....   — — —
Date of death/age ....   — — —
Cabinet service ....   — — —

Hodges, Luther H.   **CM**
Date of birth ....   Mar 9, 1898
Date of appointment/age ....   Jan 21, 1961/62
Assumed office/age ....   Jan 21, 1961/62
Left office/age ....   Jan 17, 1965/66
Date of death/age ....   Oct 6, 1974/76
Cabinet service 3y 11m 27d

Hodgson, James D.   **LB**
Date of birth ....   Dec 3, 1913
Date of appointment/age ....   Jun 10, 1970/54
Assumed office/age ....   Jul 2, 1970/54
Left office/age ....   Jan 31, 1973/57
Date of death/age ....   — — —
Cabinet service 2y 6m 29d

Holt, Joseph   **PG**
Date of birth ....   Jan 6, 1807
Date of appointment/age ....   Mar 14, 1859/52
Assumed office/age ....   Mar 14, 1859/52
Left office/age ....   Dec 31, 1860/53
Date of death/age ....   Aug 1, 1894/87
Cabinet service 1y 9m 17d

Hoover, Herbert C.   **CM**
Date of birth ....   Aug 10, 1874
Date of appointment/age ....   Mar 5, 1921/46
Assumed office/age ....   Mar 5, 1921/46
Left office/age ....   Aug 20, 1928/54
Date of death/age ....   Oct 20, 1964/90
Cabinet service 7y 5m 15d

Hopkins, Harry L.   **CM**
Date of birth ....   Aug 17, 1890
Date of appointment/age ....   Jan 23, 1939/48
Assumed office/age ....   Jan 23, 1939/48
Left office/age ....   Sep 18, 1940/50
Date of death/age ....   Jan 29, 1946/55
Cabinet service 1y 7m 26d

Houston, David F.   **AG**
Date of birth ....   Feb 17, 1866
Date of appointment/age ....   Mar 5, 1913/47
Assumed office/age ....   Mar 6, 1913/47
Left office/age ....   Feb 1, 1920/53
Date of death/age ....   Sep 2, 1940/74
Cabinet service 6y 10m 26d

Houston, David F.   **TY**
Date of birth ....   Feb 17, 1866
Date of appointment/age ....   Jan 31, 1920/53
Assumed office/age ....   Feb 2, 1920/53
Left office/age ....   Mar 3, 1921/55
Date of death/age ....   Sep 2, 1940/74
Cabinet service 1y 1m 1d

Howe, Timothy O.   **PG**
Date of birth ....   Feb 24, 1816
Date of appointment/age ....   Dec 20, 1881/65
Assumed office/age ....   Jan 5, 1882/65
Left office/age ....   Mar 25, 1883/67
Date of death/age ....   Mar 25, 1883/67
Cabinet service 1y 2m 20d

Hubbard, Samuel D.   **PG**
Date of birth ....   Aug 10, 1799
Date of appointment/age ....   Aug 31, 1852/53
Assumed office/age ....   Sep 14, 1852/53
Left office/age ....   Mar 6, 1853/53
Date of death/age ....   Oct 8, 1855/56
Cabinet service 5m 20d

Hufstedler, Shirley M.					**ED**
Date of birth			Aug 24, 1925
Date of appointment/age			Oct 30, 1979/54
Assumed office/age			Dec 1, 1979/54
Left office/age			Jan 20, 1981/55
Date of death/age			— — —
Cabinet service			1y 1m 19d

Hughes, Charles Evans					**ST**
Date of birth			Apr 11, 1862
Date of appointment/age			Mar 4, 1921/58
Assumed office/age			Mar 5, 1921/58
Left office/age			Mar 4, 1925/62
Date of death/age			Aug 27, 1948/86
Cabinet service			4y

Hull, Cordell					**ST**
Date of birth			Oct 2, 1871
Date of appointment/age			Mar 4, 1933/61
Assumed office/age			Mar 4, 1933/61
Left office/age			Nov 30, 1944/73
Date of death/age			Jul 23, 1955/83
Cabinet service			11y 8m 26d

Humphrey, George M.					**TY**
Date of birth			Mar 8, 1890
Date of appointment/age			Jan 21, 1953/62
Assumed office/age			Jan 21, 1953/62
Left office/age			Jul 28, 1957/67
Date of death/age			Jan 20, 1970/79
Cabinet service			4y 6m 7d

Hunt, William H.					**NV**
Date of birth			Jun 12, 1823
Date of appointment/age			Mar 5, 1881/57
Assumed office/age			Mar 7, 1881/57
Left office/age			Apr 16, 1882/58
Date of death/age			Feb 27, 1884/60
Cabinet service			1y 1m 9d

Hurley, Patrick J.   **WR**

Date of birth	Jan 8, 1883
Date of appointment/age	Dec 9, 1929/46
Assumed office/age	Dec 9, 1929/46
Left office/age	Mar 3, 1933/50
Date of death/age	Jul 30, 1963/80
Cabinet service	3y 2m 22d

Hyde, Arthur M.   **AG**

Date of birth	Jul 12, 1877
Date of appointment/age	Mar 5, 1929/51
Assumed office/age	Mar 6, 1929/51
Left office/age	Mar 3, 1933/55
Date of death/age	Oct 17, 1947/70
Cabinet service	3y 11m 25d

Ickes, Harold L.   **IN**

Date of birth	Mar 15, 1874
Date of appointment/age	Mar 4, 1933/58
Assumed office/age	Mar 4, 1933/58
Left office/age	Feb 15, 1946/71
Date of death/age	Feb 3, 1952/77
Cabinet service	12y 11m 11d

Ingham, Samuel D.   **TY**

Date of birth	Sep 16, 1779
Date of appointment/age	Mar 6, 1829/49
Assumed office/age	Mar 6, 1829/49
Left office/age	Jun 20, 1831/51
Date of death/age	Jun 5, 1860/80
Cabinet service	2y 3m 14d

Jackson, Robert H.   **AT**

Date of birth	Feb 13, 1892
Date of appointment/age	Jan 18, 1940/47
Assumed office/age	Jan 18, 1940/47
Left office/age	Sep 4, 1941/49
Date of death/age	Oct 9, 1954/62
Cabinet service	1y 7m 17d

James, Thomas L. PG
Date of birth . . . . Mar 29, 1831
Date of appointment/age . . . . Mar 5, 1881/49
Assumed office/age . . . . Mar 8, 1881/49
Left office/age . . . . Jan 4, 1882/50
Date of death/age . . . . Sep 11, 1916/85
Cabinet service 9m 27d

Jardine, William M. AG
Date of birth . . . . Jan 16, 1879
Date of appointment/age . . . . Feb 18, 1925/46
Assumed office/age . . . . Mar 5, 1925/46
Left office/age . . . . Mar 5, 1929/50
Date of death/age . . . . Jan 17, 1955/76
Cabinet service 4y

Jefferson, Thomas ST
Date of birth . . . . Apr 13, 1743
Date of appointment/age . . . . Sep 26, 1789/46
Assumed office/age . . . . Mar 22, 1790/46
Left office/age . . . . Jan 2, 1794/50
Date of death/age . . . . Jul 4, 1826/83
Cabinet service 3y 9m 11d

Jewell, Marshall PG
Date of birth . . . . Oct 20, 1825
Date of appointment/age . . . . Aug 24, 1874/48
Assumed office/age . . . . Sep 1, 1874/48
Left office/age . . . . Jul 11, 1876/50
Date of death/age . . . . Feb 10, 1883/57
Cabinet service 1y 10m 10d

Johnson, Cave PG
Date of birth . . . . Jan 11, 1793
Date of appointment/age . . . . Mar 6, 1845/52
Assumed office/age . . . . Mar 6, 1845/52
Left office/age . . . . Mar 5, 1849/56
Date of death/age . . . . Nov 23, 1866/73
Cabinet service 4y

Johnson, Louis A.   **DF**
Date of birth ....   Jan 10, 1891
Date of appointment/age ....   Mar 23, 1949/58
Assumed office/age ....   Mar 28, 1949/58
Left office/age ....   Sep 20, 1950/59
Date of death/age ....   Apr 24, 1966/75
Cabinet service 1y 5m 23d

Johnson, Reverdy   **AT**
Date of birth ....   May 21, 1796
Date of appointment/age ....   Mar 8, 1849/52
Assumed office/age ....   Mar 8, 1849/52
Left office/age ....   Jul 22, 1850/54
Date of death/age ....   Feb 10, 1876/79
Cabinet service 1y 4m 14d

Jones, Jesse   **CM**
Date of birth ....   Apr 5, 1874
Date of appointment/age ....   Sep 16, 1940/66
Assumed office/age ....   Sep 19, 1940/66
Left office/age ....   Mar 1, 1945/70
Date of death/age ....   Jun 1, 1956/82
Cabinet service 4y 5m 10d

Jones, William   **NV**
Date of birth   1760
Date of appointment/age ....   Jan 12, 1813/52
Assumed office/age ....   Jan 19, 1813/52
Left office/age ....   Dec 1, 1814/53
Date of death/age ....   Sep 6, 1831/70
Cabinet service 1y 10m 12d

Katzenbach, Nicholas D.   **AT**
Date of birth ....   Jan 17, 1922
Date of appointment/age ....   Feb 13, 1965/43
Assumed office/age ....   Feb 13, 1965/43
Left office/age ....   Mar 9, 1967/45
Date of death/age ....   — — —
Cabinet service 2y 23d

Kellog, Frank B.   **ST**
Date of birth ....   Dec 22, 1856
Date of appointment/age ....   Feb 16, 1925/68
Assumed office/age ....   Mar 5, 1925/68
Left office/age ....   Mar 3, 1929/72
Date of death/age ....   Dec 21, 1937/80
Cabinet service 3y 11m 28d

Kendall, Amos   **PG**
Date of birth ....   Aug 16, 1789
Date of appointment/age ....   May 1, 1835/45
Assumed office/age ....   May 1, 1835/45
Left office/age ....   May 24, 1840/50
Date of death/age ....   Nov 12, 1869/80
Cabinet service 5y 23d

Kennedy, David M.   **TY**
Date of birth ....   Jul 21, 1905
Date of appointment/age ....   Jan 20, 1969/63
Assumed office/age ....   Jan 22, 1969/63
Left office/age ....   Feb 1, 1971/65
Date of death/age ....   — — —
Cabinet service 2y 10d

Kennedy, John P.   **NV**
Date of birth ....   Oct 25, 1795
Date of appointment/age ....   Jul 22, 1852/56
Assumed office/age ....   Jul 26, 1852/56
Left office/age ....   Mar 6, 1853/57
Date of death/age ....   Aug 18, 1870/74
Cabinet service 7m 8d

Kennedy, Robert F.   **AT**
Date of birth ....   Nov 20, 1925
Date of appointment/age ....   Jan 21, 1961/35
Assumed office/age ....   Jan 21, 1961/35
Left office/age ....   Feb 12, 1965/39
Date of death/age ....   Jun 6, 1968/42
Cabinet service 4y 22d

Key, David M.   **PG**
Date of birth ....   Jan 27, 1824
Date of appointment/age ....   Mar 12, 1877/53
Assumed office/age ....   Mar 12, 1877/53
Left office/age ....   Aug 24, 1880/56
Date of death/age ....   Feb 3, 1900/76
Cabinet service 3y 5m 12d

King, Horatio   **PG**
Date of birth ....   Jun 21, 1811
Date of appointment/age ....   Feb 12, 1861/49
Assumed office/age ....   Feb 12, 1861/49
Left office/age ....   Mar 8, 1861/49
Date of death/age ....   May 20, 1897/85
Cabinet service 24d

Kirkwood, Samuel J.   **IN**
Date of birth ....   Dec 20, 1813
Date of appointment/age ....   Mar 5, 1881/67
Assumed office/age ....   Mar 8, 1881/67
Left office/age ....   Apr 16, 1882/68
Date of death/age ....   Sep 1, 1894/80
Cabinet service 1y 1m 8d

Kissinger, Henry A.   **ST**
Date of birth ....   May 27, 1923
Date of appointment/age ....   Aug 22, 1973/50
Assumed office/age ....   Sep 21, 1973/50
Left office/age ....   Jan 21, 1977/53
Date of death/age ....   — — —
Cabinet service 3y 4m

Kleindienst, Richard G.   **AT**
Date of birth ....   Aug 5, 1923
Date of appointment/age ....   Feb 22, 1972/48
Assumed office/age ....   Jun 8, 1972/48
Left office/age ....   Apr 30, 1973/49
Date of death/age ....   — — —
Cabinet service 10m 22d

Klutznik, Philip M.   **CM**
Date of birth .... Jul 9, 1907
Date of appointment/age .... Nov 17, 1979/72
Assumed office/age .... Dec 21, 1979/72
Left office/age .... Jan 20, 1981/73
Date of death/age .... — — —
Cabinet service 1y 1m

Knebel, John A.   **AG**
Date of birth .... Oct 4, 1936
Date of appointment/age .... Oct 5, 1976/40
Assumed office/age .... Oct 5, 1976/40
Left office/age .... Jan 24, 1977/40
Date of death/age .... — — —
Cabinet service 3m 19d

Kleppe, Thomas S.   **IN**
Date of birth .... Jul 1, 1919
Date of appointment/age .... Sep 5, 1975/56
Assumed office/age .... Oct 10, 1975/56
Left office/age .... Jan 20, 1977/57
Date of death/age .... — — —
Cabinet service 1y 3m 10d

Knox, Henry   **WR**
Date of birth .... Jul 25, 1750
Date of appointment/age .... Sep 12, 1789/39
Assumed office/age .... Sep 12, 1789/39
Left office/age .... Jan 1, 1795/44
Date of death/age .... Oct 25, 1806/56
Cabinet service 5y 3m 20d

Knox, Philander C.   **AT**
Date of birth .... May 6, 1853
Date of appointment/age .... Apr 5, 1901/47
Assumed office/age .... Apr 9, 1901/47
Left office/age .... Jun 30, 1904/51
Date of death/age .... Oct 12, 1921/68
Cabinet service 3y 2m 11d

Knox, Philander C.   ST

Date of birth	May 6, 1853
Date of appointment/age	Mar 5, 1909/55
Assumed office/age	Mar 5, 1909/55
Left office/age	Mar 4, 1913/59
Date of death/age	Oct 12, 1921/68
Cabinet service	4y

Knox, William Franklin   NV

Date of birth	Jan 1, 1874
Date of appointment/age	Jul 10, 1940/66
Assumed office/age	Jul 10, 1940/66
Left office/age	Apr 28, 1944/70
Date of death/age	Apr 28, 1944/70
Cabinet service	3y 9m 18d

Kreps, Juanita M.   CM

Date of birth	Jan 11, 1921
Date of appointment/age	Dec 21, 1976/55
Assumed office/age	Jan 21, 1977/56
Left office/age	Oct 31, 1979/58
Date of death/age	— — —
Cabinet service	2y 9m 10d

Krug, Julius A.   IN

Date of birth	Nov 23, 1907
Date of appointment/age	Mar 6, 1946/38
Assumed office/age	Mar 18, 1946/38
Left office/age	Nov 30, 1949/42
Date of death/age	Mar 26, 1970/62
Cabinet service	3y 8m 12d

Laird, Melvin R.   DF

Date of birth	Sep 1, 1922
Date of appointment/age	Jan 20, 1969/46
Assumed office/age	Jan 22, 1969/46
Left office/age	Jan 20, 1973/50
Date of death/age	— — —
Cabinet service	3y 11m 26d

Lamar, Lucius Q.C.   **IN**
Date of birth ....   Sep 17, 1825
Date of appointment/age ....   Mar 6, 1885/59
Assumed office/age ....   Mar 6, 1885/59
Left office/age ....   Jan 10, 1888/62
Date of death/age ....   Jan 23, 1893/67
Cabinet service 2y 10m 4d

Lamont, Daniel S.   **WR**
Date of birth ....   Feb 9, 1851
Date of appointment/age ....   Mar 6, 1893/42
Assumed office/age ....   Mar 6, 1893/42
Left office/age ....   Mar 4, 1897/46
Date of death/age ....   Jul 23, 1905/54
Cabinet service 3y 11m 28d

Lamont, Robert P.   **CM**
Date of birth ....   Dec 1, 1867
Date of appointment/age ....   Mar 5, 1929/61
Assumed office/age ....   Mar 5, 1929/61
Left office/age ....   Aug 7, 1932/64
Date of death/age ....   Feb 19, 1948/80
Cabinet service 3y 5m 2d

Landrieu, Moon   **HD**
Date of birth ....   Jul 23, 1930
Date of appointment/age ....   Jul 28, 1979/49
Assumed office/age ....   Sep 25, 1979/49
Left office/age ....   Jan 20, 1981/50
Date of death/age ....   — — —
Cabinet service 1y 3m 26d

Lane, Franklin K.   **IN**
Date of birth ....   Jul 15, 1864
Date of appointment/age ....   Mar 5, 1913/48
Assumed office/age ....   Mar 5, 1913/48
Left office/age ....   Mar 12, 1920/55
Date of death/age ....   May 18, 1921/56
Cabinet service 8y 2m 13d

Lansing, Robert   **ST**
Date of birth . . . . Oct 17, 1864
Date of appointment/age . . . . Jun 23, 1915/50
Assumed office/age . . . . Jun 23, 1915/50
Left office/age . . . . Feb 13, 1920/55
Date of death/age . . . . Oct 30, 1928/64
Cabinet service 4y 7m 21d

Lee, Charles   **AT**
Date of birth   1758
Date of appointment/age . . . . Nov 30, 1795/36
Assumed office/age . . . . Dec 10, 1795/36
Left office/age . . . . Mar 4, 1801/42
Date of death/age . . . . Jun 24, 1815/56
Cabinet service 5y 2m 22d

Legare, Hugh S.   **AT**
Date of birth . . . . Jan 2, 1797
Date of appointment/age . . . . Sep 20, 1841/44
Assumed office/age . . . . Sep 20, 1841/44
Left office/age . . . . Jun 20, 1843/46
Date of death/age . . . . Jun 20, 1843/46
Cabinet service 1y 9m

Levi, Edward H.   **AT**
Date of birth . . . . Jun 26, 1911
Date of appointment/age . . . . Jan 15, 1975/64
Assumed office/age . . . . Feb 6, 1975/64
Left office/age . . . . Jan 20, 1977/65
Date of death/age . . . . — — —
Cabinet service 1y 11m 14d

Lewis, Andrew L., Jr.   **TR**
Date of birth . . . . Nov 3, 1931
Date of appointment/age . . . . Dec 12, 1980/49
Assumed office/age . . . . Jan 23, 1981/49
Left office/age . . . . Feb 1, 1983/51
Date of death/age . . . . — — —
Cabinet service 2y 9d

Lincoln, Levi   **AT**
Date of birth ....   May 15, 1749
Date of appointment/age ....   Mar 5, 1801/51
Assumed office/age ....   Mar 5, 1801/51
Left office/age ....   Dec 31, 1804/55
Date of death/age ....   Apr 14, 1820/70
Cabinet service 3y 9m 26d

Lincoln, Robert T.   **WR**
Date of birth ....   Aug 1, 1843
Date of appointment/age ....   Mar 5, 1881/37
Assumed office/age ....   Mar 11, 1881/37
Left office/age ....   Mar 5, 1885/41
Date of death/age ....   Jul 26, 1926/82
Cabinet service 3y 11m 24d

Livingston, Edward   **ST**
Date of birth ....   May 28, 1764
Date of appointment/age ....   May 24, 1831/66
Assumed office/age ....   May 24, 1831/66
Left office/age ....   May 28, 1833/69
Date of death/age ....   May 23, 1836/71
Cabinet service 2y 4d

Long, John D.   **NV**
Date of birth ....   Oct 27, 1838
Date of appointment/age ....   Mar 5, 1897/58
Assumed office/age ....   Mar 5, 1897/58
Left office/age ....   Apr 30, 1902/63
Date of death/age ....   Aug 28, 1915/76
Cabinet service 5y 1m 25d

Lovett, Robert A.   **DF**
Date of birth ....   Sep 14, 1895
Date of appointment/age ....   Sep 14, 1951/56
Assumed office/age ....   Sep 17, 1951/56
Left office/age ....   Jan 20, 1953/57
Date of death/age ....   — — —
Cabinet service 1y 4m 10d

Lynn, James T.   **HD**
Date of birth . . . .   Apr 27, 1927
Date of appointment/age . . . .   Dec 6, 1972/45
Assumed office/age . . . .   Jan 31, 1973/45
Left office/age . . . .   Jan 1, 1975/47
Date of death/age . . . .   — — —
Cabinet service 1y 11m 1d

McAdoo, William G.   **TY**
Date of birth . . . .   Oct 31, 1863
Date of appointment/age . . . .   Mar 5, 1913/49
Assumed office/age . . . .   Mar 6, 1913/49
Left office/age . . . .   Dec 15, 1918/55
Date of death/age . . . .   Feb 1, 1941/77
Cabinet service 5y 9m 9d

McClelland, Robert   **IN**
Date of birth . . . .   Aug 1, 1807
Date of appointment/age . . . .   Mar 7, 1853/45
Assumed office/age . . . .   Mar 7, 1853/45
Left office/age . . . .   Mar 9, 1857/49
Date of death/age . . . .   Aug 30, 1880/73
Cabinet service 4y 2d

McCrary, George W.   **WR**
Date of birth . . . .   Aug 29, 1835
Date of appointment/age . . . .   Mar 12, 1877/41
Assumed office/age . . . .   Mar 12, 1877/41
Left office/age . . . .   Dec 11, 1879/44
Date of death/age . . . .   Jun 23, 1890/54
Cabinet service 2y 8m 29d

McCulloch, Hugh   **TY**
Date of birth . . . .   Dec 7, 1808
Date of appointment/age . . . .   Mar 7, 1865/56
Assumed office/age . . . .   Mar 9, 1865/56
Left office/age . . . .   Mar 4, 1869/60
Date of death/age . . . .   May 24, 1895/86
Cabinet service 3y 11m 25d

McCulloch, Hugh   **TY**
Date of birth .... Dec 7, 1808
Date of appointment/age .... Oct 28, 1884/75
Assumed office/age .... Oct 31, 1884/75
Left office/age .... Mar 7, 1885/76
Date of death/age .... May 24, 1895/86
Cabinet service 4m 7d

McElroy, Neil H.   **DF**
Date of birth .... Oct 30, 1904
Date of appointment/age .... Aug 19, 1957/52
Assumed office/age .... Oct 9, 1957/52
Left office/age .... Dec 1, 1960/56
Date of death/age .... Nov 30, 1972/68
Cabinet service 3y 3m 11d

McGrath, J. Howard   **AT**
Date of birth .... Nov 28, 1903
Date of appointment/age .... Aug 19, 1949/45
Assumed office/age .... Aug 24, 1949/45
Left office/age .... Jan 20, 1953/49
Date of death/age .... Sep 2, 1966/62
Cabinet service 3y 4m 27d

McHenry, James   **WR**
Date of birth .... Nov 16, 1753
Date of appointment/age .... Jan 27, 1796/42
Assumed office/age .... Feb 6, 1796/42
Left office/age .... May 31, 1800/46
Date of death/age .... May 3, 1816/62
Cabinet service 4y 3m 25d

McKay, Douglas   **IN**
Date of birth .... Jun 24, 1893
Date of appointment/age .... Jan 21, 1953/59
Assumed office/age .... Jan 21, 1953/59
Left office/age .... Jun 7, 1956/61
Date of death/age .... Jul 22, 1959/66
Cabinet service 3y 4m 17d

McKenna, Joseph   **AT**
Date of birth ....   Aug 10, 1843
Date of appointment/age ....   Mar 5, 1897/53
Assumed office/age ....   Mar 7, 1897/53
Left office/age ....   Jan 25, 1898/54
Date of death/age ....   Nov 21, 1926/83
Cabinet service 10m 18d

McKennan, Thomas M.T.   **IN**
Date of birth ....   Mar 31, 1794
Date of appointment/age ....   Aug 15, 1850/56
Assumed office/age ....   Aug 15, 1850/56
Left office/age ....   Aug 26, 1850/56
Date of death/age ....   Jul 9, 1852/58
Cabinet service 11d

McLane, Louis   **TY**
Date of birth ....   May 28, 1786
Date of appointment/age ....   Aug 8, 1831/45
Assumed office/age ....   Aug 8, 1831/45
Left office/age ....   May 31, 1833/47
Date of death/age ....   Oct 7, 1857/71
Cabinet service 1y 9m 23d

McLane, Louis   **ST**
Date of birth ....   May 28, 1786
Date of appointment/age ....   May 29, 1833/47
Assumed office/age ....   May 29, 1833/47
Left office/age ....   Jun 30, 1834/48
Date of death/age ....   Oct 7, 1857/71
Cabinet service 1y 1m 1d

McLean, John   **PG**
Date of birth ....   Mar 11, 1785
Date of appointment/age ....   Jun 26, 1823/38
Assumed office/age ....   Jul 1, 1823/38
Left office/age ....   Apr 5, 1829/44
Date of death/age ....   Apr 4, 1861/76
Cabinet service 5y 9m 4d

McNamara, Robert S.   **DF**
Date of birth ....   Jun 9, 1916
Date of appointment/age ....   Jan 21, 1961/44
Assumed office/age ....   Jan 21, 1961/44
Left office/age ....   Feb 29, 1968/51
Date of death/age ....   — — —
Cabinet service 7y 1m 8d

McReynolds, James C.   **AT**
Date of birth ....   Feb 3, 1862
Date of appointment/age ....   Mar 5, 1913/51
Assumed office/age ....   Mar 6, 1913/51
Left office/age ....   Sep 2, 1914/52
Date of death/age ....   Aug 24, 1946/84
Cabinet service 1y 5m 27d

MacVeagh, Franklin   **TY**
Date of birth ....   Nov 22, 1837
Date of appointment/age ....   Mar 5, 1909/71
Assumed office/age ....   Mar 8, 1909/71
Left office/age ....   Mar 5, 1913/75
Date of death/age ....   Jul 6, 1934/96
Cabinet service 3y 11m 27d

McVeagh, Isaac Wayne   **AT**
Date of birth ....   Apr 19, 1833
Date of appointment/age ....   Mar 5, 1881/47
Assumed office/age ....   Mar 7, 1881/47
Left office/age ....   Nov 13, 1881/48
Date of death/age ....   Jan 11, 1917/83
Cabinet service 8m 6d

Madison, James   **ST**
Date of birth ....   Mar 16, 1751
Date of appointment/age ....   Mar 5, 1801/49
Assumed office/age ....   May 2, 1801/50
Left office/age ....   Mar 3, 1809/57
Date of death/age ....   Jun 28, 1836/85
Cabinet service 7y 10m 1d

Manning, Daniel   **TY**
Date of birth ....   May 16, 1831
Date of appointment/age ....   Mar 6, 1885/53
Assumed office/age ....   Mar 8, 1885/53
Left office/age ....   Mar 31, 1887/55
Date of death/age ....   Dec 24, 1887/56
Cabinet service 2y 23d

Marcy, William L.   **WR**
Date of birth ....   Dec 12, 1786
Date of appointment/age ....   Mar 6, 1845/58
Assumed office/age ....   Mar 8, 1845/58
Left office/age ....   Mar 7, 1849/62
Date of death/age ....   Jul 4, 1857/70
Cabinet service 3y 11m 29d

Marcy, William L.   **ST**
Date of birth ....   Dec 12, 1786
Date of appointment/age ....   Mar 7, 1853/66
Assumed office/age ....   Mar 7, 1853/66
Left office/age ....   Mar 5, 1857/70
Date of death/age ....   Jul 4, 1857/70
Cabinet service 3y 11m 28d

Marshall, F. Ray   **LB**
Date of birth ....   Aug 22, 1928
Date of appointment/age ....   Dec 22, 1976/48
Assumed office/age ....   Jan 27, 1977/48
Left office/age ....   Jan 20, 1981/52
Date of death/age ....   — — —
Cabinet service 3y 11m 24d

Marshall, George C., Jr.   **ST**
Date of birth ....   Dec 31, 1880
Date of appointment/age ....   Jan 8, 1947/66
Assumed office/age ....   Jan 21, 1947/66
Left office/age ....   Jan 20, 1949/68
Date of death/age ....   Oct 16, 1959/78
Cabinet service 2y

Marshall, George C., Jr.　　　　　**DF**
Date of birth .... Dec 31, 1880
Date of appointment/age .... Sep 21, 1950/69
Assumed office/age .... Sep 21, 1850/69
Left office/age .... Sep 16, 1951/70
Date of death/age .... Oct 16, 1959/78
Cabinet service 11m 25d

Marshall, John　　　　　**ST**
Date of birth .... Sep 24, 1755
Date of appointment/age .... May 13, 1800/44
Assumed office/age .... Jun 6, 1800/44
Left office/age .... Feb 4, 1801/45
Date of death/age .... Jul 6, 1835/79
Cabinet service 7m 29d

Mason, John Y.　　　　　**NV**
Date of birth .... Apr 18, 1799
Date of appointment/age .... Mar 14, 1844/44
Assumed office/age .... Mar 26, 1844/44
Left office/age .... Mar 9, 1845/45
Date of death/age .... Oct 3, 1859/60
Cabinet service 11m 11d

Mason, John Y.　　　　　**AT**
Date of birth .... Apr 18, 1799
Date of appointment/age .... Mar 4, 1845/45
Assumed office/age .... Mar 11, 1845/45
Left office/age .... Sep 9, 1846/47
Date of death/age .... Oct 3, 1859/60
Cabinet service 1y 5m 29d

Mason, John Y.　　　　　**NV**
Date of birth .... Apr 18, 1799
Date of appointment/age .... Sep 9, 1846/47
Assumed office/age .... Sep 9, 1846/47
Left office/age .... Mar 7, 1849/49
Date of death/age .... Oct 3, 1859/60
Cabinet service 2y 5m 26d

Mathews, Forrest D.   **HW**

Date of birth	Dec 6, 1935
Date of appointment/age	Jun 27, 1975/39
Assumed office/age	Jul 23, 1975/39
Left office/age	Jan 20, 1977/41
Date of death/age	— — —
Cabinet service	1y 5m 28d

Maynard, Horace   **PG**

Date of birth	Aug 30, 1814
Date of appointment/age	Jun 2, 1880/65
Assumed office/age	Aug 25, 1880/65
Left office/age	Mar 7, 1881/66
Date of death/age	May 3, 1882/67
Cabinet service	6m 10d

Meese, Edwin L.   **AT**

Date of birth	1931
Date of appointment/age	Jan 10, 1985/54
Assumed office/age	Feb 23, 1985/54
Left office/age	— — —
Date of death/age	— — —
Cabinet service	— — —

Meigs, Return J., Jr.   **PG**

Date of birth	Nov 17, 1764
Date of appointment/age	Mar 17, 1814/49
Assumed office/age	Apr 11, 1814/49
Left office/age	Jun 30, 1823/58
Date of death/age	Mar 29, 1824/59
Cabinet service	9y 2m 19d

Mellon, Andrew W.   **TY**

Date of birth	Mar 24, 1855
Date of appointment/age	Mar 4, 1921/65
Assumed office/age	Mar 5, 1921/65
Left office/age	Feb 12, 1932/76
Date of death/age	Aug 26, 1937/82
Cabinet service	10y 11m 7d

Meredith, Edwin T.   **AG**
Date of birth ....   Dec 23, 1876
Date of appointment/age ....   Jan 31, 1920/43
Assumed office/age ....   Feb 2, 1920/43
Left office/age ....   Mar 4, 1921/44
Date of death/age ....   Jun 17, 1928/51
Cabinet service 1y 1m 2d

Meredith, William M.   **TY**
Date of birth ....   Jun 8, 1799
Date of appointment/age ....   Mar 8, 1849/49
Assumed office/age ....   Mar 8, 1849/49
Left office/age ....   Jul 22, 1850/50
Date of death/age ....   Aug 17, 1873/74
Cabinet service 1y 4m 14d

Metcalf, Victor H.   **CL**
Date of birth ....   Oct 10, 1853
Date of appointment/age ....   Jul 1, 1904/50
Assumed office/age ....   Jul 1, 1904/50
Left office/age ....   Dec 16, 1906/53
Date of death/age ....   Feb 20, 1936/82
Cabinet service 2y 5m 15d

Metcalf, Victor H.   **NV**
Date of birth ....   Oct 10, 1853
Date of appointment/age ....   Dec 12, 1906/53
Assumed office/age ....   Dec 17, 1906/53
Left office/age ....   Nov 30, 1908/55
Date of death/age ....   Feb 20, 1936/82
Cabinet service 1y 11m 13d

Meyer, George von L.   **PG**
Date of birth ....   Jun 24, 1858
Date of appointment/age ....—...   Jan 15, 1907/48
Assumed office/age ....   Mar 4, 1907/48
Left office/age ....   Mar 4, 1909/50
Date of death/age ....   Mar 9, 1918/59
Cabinet service 2y

Meyer, George von L.   **NV**
Date of birth . . . .   Jun 24, 1858
Date of appointment/age . . . .   Mar 5, 1909/50
Assumed office/age . . . .   Mar 5, 1909/50
Left office/age . . . .   Mar 4, 1913/54
Date of death/age . . . .   Mar 9, 1918/59
Cabinet service 4y

Miller, G. William   **TY**
Date of birth . . . .   Mar 9, 1925
Date of appointment/age . . . .   Jul 20, 1979/54
Assumed office/age . . . .   Aug 3, 1979/54
Left office/age . . . .   Jan 20, 1981/55
Date of death/age . . . .   — — —
Cabinet service 1y 5m 17d

Marshall, James William   **PG**
Date of birth . . . .   Aug 14, 1822
Date of appointment/age . . . .   Jul 3, 1874/51
Assumed office/age . . . .   Jul 7, 1874/51
Left office/age . . . .   Aug 24, 1874/52
Date of death/age . . . .   Feb 5, 1910/87
Cabinet service 1m 24d

Miller, William H.H.   **AT**
Date of birth . . . .   Sep 6, 1840
Date of appointment/age . . . .   Mar 5, 1889/48
Assumed office/age . . . .   Mar 5, 1889/48
Left office/age . . . .   Mar 5, 1893/52
Date of death/age . . . .   May 25, 1917/76
Cabinet service 4y

Mills, Ogden L.   **TY**
Date of birth . . . .   Aug 23, 1884
Date of appointment/age . . . .   Feb 10, 1932/47
Assumed office/age . . . .   Feb 13, 1932/47
Left office/age . . . .   Mar 3, 1933/48
Date of death/age . . . .   Oct 11, 1937/53
Cabinet service 1y 18d

Mitchell, James P.   **LB**
Date of birth ....   Nov 12, 1900
Date of appointment/age ....   Oct 9, 1953/52
Assumed office/age ....   Oct 9, 1953/52
Left office/age ....   Jan 20, 1961/60
Date of death/age ....   Oct 19, 1964/63
Cabinet service 7y 3m 11d

Mitchell, John N.   **AT**
Date of birth ....   Sep 15, 1913
Date of appointment/age ....   Jan 20, 1969/55
Assumed office/age ....   Jan 22, 1969/55
Left office/age ....   Feb 16, 1972/58
Date of death/age ....   — — —
Cabinet service 3y 25d

Mitchell, William D.   **AT**
Date of birth ....   Sep 9, 1874
Date of appointment/age ....   Mar 5, 1929/54
Assumed office/age ....   Mar 6, 1929/54
Left office/age ....   Mar 3, 1933/58
Date of death/age ....   Aug 24, 1955/80
Cabinet service 3y 11m 27d

Monroe, James   **ST**
Date of birth ....   Apr 28, 1758
Date of appointment/age ....   Apr 2, 1811/52
Assumed office/age ....   Apr 6, 1811/52
Left office/age ....   Mar 3, 1817/58
Date of death/age ....   Jul 4, 1831/73
Cabinet service 5y 10m 25d

Monroe, James   **WR**
Date of birth ....   Apr 28, 1758
Date of appointment/age ....   Sep 27, 1814/56
Assumed office/age ....   Oct 1, 1814/56
Left office/age ....   Feb 28, 1815/56
Date of death/age ....   Jul 4, 1831/73
Cabinet service 4m 27d

Moody, William H.   **NV**
Date of birth .... Dec 23, 1853
Date of appointment/age .... Apr 29, 1902/48
Assumed office/age .... May 1, 1902/48
Left office/age .... Jul 1, 1904/50
Date of death/age .... Jul 2, 1917/63
Cabinet service 2y

Moody, William H.   **AT**
Date of birth .... Dec 23, 1853
Date of appointment/age .... Jul 1, 1904/50
Assumed office/age .... Jul 1, 1904/50
Left office/age .... Dec 16, 1906/52
Date of death/age .... Jul 2, 1917/63
Cabinet service 2y 5m 15d

Morgenthau, Henry, Jr.   **TY**
Date of birth .... May 11, 1891
Date of appointment/age .... Jan 8, 1934/42
Assumed office/age .... Jan 8, 1934/42
Left office/age .... Jul 22, 1945/54
Date of death/age .... Feb 6, 1967/75
Cabinet service 11y 6m 14d

Morrill, Lot M.   **TY**
Date of birth .... May 3, 1812
Date of appointment/age .... Jun 21, 1876/64
Assumed office/age .... Jul 7, 1876/64
Left office/age .... Mar 9, 1877/64
Date of death/age .... Jan 10, 1883/70
Cabinet service 8m 2d

Morton, J. Sterling   **AG**
Date of birth .... Apr 22, 1832
Date of appointment/age .... Mar 6, 1893/60
Assumed office/age .... Mar 6, 1893/60
Left office/age .... Mar 4, 1897/64
Date of death/age .... Apr 27, 1902/70
Cabinet service 3y 11m 26d

Morton, Paul   **NV**
Date of birth ....   May 22, 1857
Date of appointment/age ....   Jul 1, 1904/47
Assumed office/age ....   Jul 1, 1904/47
Left office/age ....   Jun 30, 1905/48
Date of death/age ....   Jan 20, 1911/53
Cabinet service 1y

Morton, Rogers C.B.   **CM**
Date of birth ....   Sep 19, 1914
Date of appointment/age ....   Mar 28, 1975/60
Assumed office/age ....   Apr 26, 1975/60
Left office/age ....   Dec 11, 1975/61
Date of death/age ....   Apr 19, 1979/64
Cabinet service 7m 15d

Morton, Rogers C.B.   **IN**
Date of birth ....   Sep 19, 1914
Date of appointment/age ....   Nov 25, 1970/56
Assumed office/age ....   Jan 29, 1971/56
Left office/age ....   Apr 30, 1975/60
Date of death/age ....   Apr 19, 1979/64
Cabinet service 4y 3m 1d

Mueller, Frederick H.   **CM**
Date of birth ....   Nov 22, 1893
Date of appointment/age ....   Aug 10, 1959/65
Assumed office/age ....   Aug 10, 1959/65
Left office/age ....   Jan 20, 1961/67
Date of death/age ....   Aug 31, 1976/82
Cabinet service 1y 5m 10d

Murphy, Frank   **AT**
Date of birth ....   Apr 13, 1890
Date of appointment/age ....   Jan 17, 1939/48
Assumed office/age ....   Jan 17, 1939/48
Left office/age ....   Jan 17, 1940/49
Date of death/age ....   Jul 19, 1949/59
Cabinet service 1y

Muskie, Edmund S.   ST
Date of birth .... Mar 28, 1914
Date of appointment/age .... Apr 30, 1980/66
Assumed office/age .... May 8, 1980/66
Left office/age .... Jan 20, 1981/66
Date of death/age .... — — —
Cabinet service 8m 12d

Nagel, Charles   CL
Date of birth .... Aug 9, 1849
Date of appointment/age .... Mar 5, 1909/59
Assumed office/age .... Mar 5, 1909/59
Left office/age .... Mar 4, 1913/63
Date of death/age .... Jan 5, 1940/90
Cabinet service 4y

Nelson, John   AT
Date of birth .... Jun 1, 1794
Date of appointment/age .... Jul 1, 1843/49
Assumed office/age .... Jul 1, 1843/49
Left office/age .... Mar 10, 1845/50
Date of death/age .... Jan 18, 1860/65
Cabinet service 1y 8m 9d

New, Harry S.   PG
Date of birth .... Dec 31, 1858
Date of appointment/age .... Feb 27, 1923/64
Assumed office/age .... Mar 5, 1923/64
Left office/age .... Mar 5, 1929/70
Date of death/age .... May 9, 1937/78
Cabinet service 6y

Newberry, Truman H.   NV
Date of birth .... Nov 5, 1864
Date of appointment/age .... Dec 1, 1908/44
Assumed office/age .... Dec 1, 1908/44
Left office/age .... Mar 4, 1909/44
Date of death/age .... Oct 3, 1945/80
Cabinet service 3m 3d

Niles, John M.   **PG**
Date of birth ....   Aug 20, 1787
Date of appointment/age ....   May 19, 1840/52
Assumed office/age ....   May 25, 1840/52
Left office/age ....   Mar 3, 1841/53
Date of death/age ....   May 31, 1856/68
Cabinet service 9m 6d

Noble, John W.   **IN**
Date of birth ....   Oct 26, 1831
Date of appointment/age ....   Mar 5, 1889/57
Assumed office/age ....   Mar 7, 1889/57
Left office/age ....   Mar 5, 1893/61
Date of death/age ....   Mar 22, 1912/80
Cabinet service 3y 11m 26d

O'Brien, Lawrence F.   **PG**
Date of birth ....   Jul 7, 1917
Date of appointment/age ....   Nov 3, 1965/48
Assumed office/age ....   Nov 3, 1965/48
Left office/age ....   Apr 10, 1968/50
Date of death/age ....   — — —
Cabinet service 2y 5m 7d

Olney, Richard   **AT**
Date of birth ....   Sep 15, 1835
Date of appointment/age ....   Mar 6, 1893/57
Assumed office/age ....   Mar 6, 1893/57
Left office/age ....   Jun 10, 1895/59
Date of death/age ....   Apr 8, 1917/81
Cabinet service 2y 3m 4d

Olney, Richard   **ST**
Date of birth ....   Sep 15, 1835
Date of appointment/age ....—...   Jun 8, 1895/59
Assumed office/age ....   Jun 10, 1895/59
Left office/age ....   Mar 4, 1897/61
Date of death/age ....   Apr 8, 1917/81
Cabinet service 1y 8m 22d

Osgood, Samuel   **PG**
Date of birth ....   Feb 3, 1747
Date of appointment/age ....   Sep 26, 1789/42
Assumed office/age ....   Sep 26, 1789/42
Left office/age ....   Aug 18, 1791/44
Date of death/age ....   Aug 12, 1813/66
Cabinet service 1y 10m 23d

Palmer, Alexander Mitchell   **AT**
Date of birth ....   May 4, 1872
Date of appointment/age ....   Mar 5, 1919/46
Assumed office/age ....   Mar 5, 1919/46
Left office/age ....   Mar 4, 1921/48
Date of death/age ....   May 11, 1936/64
Cabinet service 2y

Patterson, Robert P.   **WR**
Date of birth ....   Feb 12, 1891
Date of appointment/age ....   Sep 26, 1945/54
Assumed office/age ....   Sep 27, 1945/54
Left office/age ....   Jul 24, 1947/56
Date of death/age ....   Jan 22, 1952/60
Cabinet service 1y 9m 27d

Paulding, James K.   **NV**
Date of birth ....   Aug 22, 1778
Date of appointment/age ....   Jun 25, 1838/59
Assumed office/age ....   Jul 1, 1838/59
Left office/age ....   Mar 3, 1841/62
Date of death/age ....   Apr 6, 1860/81
Cabinet service 2y 8m 2d

Payne, Henry C.   **PG**
Date of birth ....   Nov 23, 1843
Date of appointment/age ....   Jan 9, 1902/58
Assumed office/age ....   Jan 9, 1902/58
Left office/age ....   Oct 4, 1904/60
Date of death/age ....   Oct 4, 1904/60
Cabinet service 2y 9m

Payne, John B.   **IN**
Date of birth ....   Jan 26, 1855
Date of appointment/age ....   Feb 28, 1920/65
Assumed office/age ....   Mar 13, 1920/65
Left office/age ....   Mar 4, 1921/66
Date of death/age ....   Jan 24, 1935/79
Cabinet service 11m 19d

Perkins, Frances   **LB**
Date of birth ....   Apr 10, 1880
Date of appointment/age ....   Mar 4, 1933/52
Assumed office/age ....   Mar 4, 1933/52
Left office/age ....   Jun 30, 1945/65
Date of death/age ....   May 14, 1965/85
Cabinet service 12y 3m 26d

Peterson, Peter G.   **CM**
Date of birth ....   Jun 5, 1926
Date of appointment/age ....   Jan 28, 1972/45
Assumed office/age ....   Feb 22, 1972/45
Left office/age ....   Jan 18, 1973/46
Date of death/age ....   — — —
Cabinet service 10m 27d

Pickering, Timothy   **PG**
Date of birth ....   Jul 17, 1745
Date of appointment/age ....   Aug 12, 1791/46
Assumed office/age ....   Aug 19, 1791/46
Left office/age ....   Feb 24, 1795/49
Date of death/age ....   Jan 29, 1829/83
Cabinet service 3y 6m 5d

Pickering, Timothy   **WR**
Date of birth ....   Jul 17, 1745
Date of appointment/age ....   Jan 2, 1795/49
Assumed office/age ....   Jan 2, 1795/49
Left office/age ....   Dec 9, 1795/50
Date of death/age ....   Jan 29, 1829/83
Cabinet service 11m 7d

Pickering, Timothy   **ST**
Date of birth ....   Jul 17, 1745
Date of appointment/age ....   Dec 10, 1795/50
Assumed office/age ....   Dec 10, 1795/50
Left office/age ....   May 12, 1800/54
Date of death/age ....   Jan 29, 1829/83
Cabinet service 4y 5m 2d

Pierce, Samuel R., Jr.   **HD**
Date of birth ....   Sep 8, 1922
Date of appointment/age ....   Dec 23, 1980/58
Assumed office/age ....   Jan 23, 1981/58
Left office/age ....   — — —
Date of death/age ....   — — —
Cabinet service ....   — — —

Pierrepont, Edwards   **AT**
Date of birth ....   Mar 4, 1817
Date of appointment/age ....   Apr 26, 1875/58
Assumed office/age ....   May 15, 1875/58
Left office/age ....   May 31, 1876/59
Date of death/age ....   Mar 6, 1892/75
Cabinet service 1y 16d

Pinkney, William   **AT**
Date of birth ....   Mar 17, 1764
Date of appointment/age ....   Dec 11, 1811/47
Assumed office/age ....   Jan 6, 1812/47
Left office/age ....   Feb 10, 1814/49
Date of death/age ....   Feb 25, 1822/57
Cabinet service 2y 1m 4d

Poinsett, Joel R.   **WR**
Date of birth ....   Mar 2, 1779
Date of appointment/age ....   Mar 7, 1837/58
Assumed office/age ....   Mar 14, 1837/58
Left office/age ....   Mar 4, 1841/62
Date of death/age ....   Dec 12, 1851/72
Cabinet service 3y 11m 20d

Porter, James M. WR
Date of birth .... Jan 6, 1793
Date of appointment/age .... Mar 8, 1843/50
Assumed office/age .... Mar 8, 1843/50
Left office/age .... Feb 19, 1844/51
Date of death/age .... Nov 11, 1862/69
Cabinet service 11m 11d

Porter, Peter B. WR
Date of birth .... Aug 14, 1773
Date of appointment/age .... May 26, 1828/54
Assumed office/age .... Jun 21, 1828/54
Left office/age .... Mar 3, 1829/55
Date of death/age .... Mar 20, 1844/70
Cabinet service 8m 10d

Preston, William B. NV
Date of birth .... Nov 29, 1805
Date of appointment/age .... Mar 8, 1849/43
Assumed office/age .... Mar 8, 1849/43
Left office/age .... Jul 22, 1850/44
Date of death/age .... Nov 16, 1862/56
Cabinet service 1y 4m 14d

Proctor, Redfield WR
Date of birth .... Jun 1, 1831
Date of appointment/age .... Mar 5, 1889/57
Assumed office/age .... Mar 5, 1889/57
Left office/age .... Dec 5, 1891/60
Date of death/age .... Mar 4, 1908/76
Cabinet service 2y 9m

Ramsey, Alexander WR
Date of birth .... Sep 8, 1815
Date of appointment/age .... Dec 10, 1879/64
Assumed office/age .... Dec 12, 1879/64
Left office/age .... Mar 10, 1881/65
Date of death/age .... Apr 22, 1903/87
Cabinet service 1y 2m 26d

Randall, Alexander W.   PG

Date of birth	Oct 31, 1819
Date of appointment/age	Jul 25, 1866/46
Assumed office/age	Jul 25, 1866/46
Left office/age	Mar 3, 1869/49
Date of death/age	Jul 26, 1872/52
Cabinet service	2y 7m 6d

Randolph, Edmund   AT

Date of birth	Aug 10, 1753
Date of appointment/age	Sep 26, 1789/36
Assumed office/age	Feb 2, 1790/36
Left office/age	Jan 28, 1794/40
Date of death/age	Sep 12, 1813/60
Cabinet service	3y 11m 26d

Randolph, Edmund   ST

Date of birth	Aug 10, 1753
Date of appointment/age	Jan 2, 1794/40
Assumed office/age	Jan 2, 1794/40
Left office/age	Aug 20, 1795/42
Date of death/age	Sep 12, 1813/60
Cabinet service	1y 7m 18d

Rawlins, John A.   WR

Date of birth	Feb 13, 1831
Date of appointment/age	Mar 11, 1869/38
Assumed office/age	Mar 11, 1869/38
Left office/age	Sep 6, 1869/38
Date of death/age	Sep 6, 1869/38
Cabinet service	5m 25d

Redfield, William C.   CM

Date of birth	Jun 18, 1858
Date of appointment/age	Mar 5, 1913/54
Assumed office/age	Mar 5, 1913/54
Left office/age	Dec 15, 1919/61
Date of death/age	Jun 13, 1932/73
Cabinet service	6y 9m 10d

Regan, Donald T.   **TY**
Date of birth ....   Dec 21, 1918
Date of appointment/age ....   Dec 12, 1980/61
Assumed office/age ....   Jan 22, 1981/62
Left office/age ....   Jan 29, 1985/66
Date of death/age ....   — — —
Cabinet service 4y 7d

Ribicoff, Abraham A.   **HW**
Date of birth ....   Apr 9, 1910
Date of appointment/age ....   Jan 21, 1961/50
Assumed office/age ....   Jan 21, 1961/50
Left office/age ....   Jul 30, 1962/52
Date of death/age ....   — — —
Cabinet service 1y 6m 9d

Richardson, Elliot L.   **HW**
Date of birth ....   Jul 20, 1920
Date of appointment/age ....   Jun 7, 1970/49
Assumed office/age ....   Jun 16, 1970/49
Left office/age ....   Jan 20, 1973/52
Date of death/age ....   — — —
Cabinet service 2y 7m 4d

Richardson, Elliot L.   **DF**
Date of birth ....   Jul 20, 1920
Date of appointment/age ....   Nov 28, 1972/52
Assumed office/age ....   Jan 29, 1973/52
Left office/age ....   Apr 30, 1973/52
Date of death/age ....   — — —
Cabinet service 3m 1d

Richardson, Elliot L.   **AT**
Date of birth ....   Jul 20, 1920
Date of appointment/age ....   Apr 30, 1973/52
Assumed office/age ....   May 23, 1973/52
Left office/age ....   Oct 20, 1973/53
Date of death/age ....   — — —
Cabinet service 4m 27d

Richardson, Elliot L.   **CM**

Date of birth	Jul 20, 1920
Date of appointment/age	Nov 4, 1975/55
Assumed office/age	Dec 11, 1975/55
Left office/age	Jan 20, 1977/56
Date of death/age	— — —
Cabinet service	1y 1m 9d

Richardson, William A.   **TY**

Date of birth	Nov 2, 1821
Date of appointment/age	Mar 17, 1873/51
Assumed office/age	Mar 17, 1873/51
Left office/age	Jun 3, 1874/52
Date of death/age	Oct 19, 1896/74
Cabinet service	1y 2m 17d

Robeson, George M.   **NV**

Date of birth	Mar 16, 1829
Date of appointment/age	Jun 25, 1869/40
Assumed office/age	Jun 25, 1869/40
Left office/age	Mar 11, 1877/47
Date of death/age	Sep 27, 1897/68
Cabinet service	7y 8m 14d

Rodney, Caesar A.   **AT**

Date of birth	Jan 4, 1772
Date of appointment/age	Jan 20, 1807/35
Assumed office/age	Jan 20, 1807/35
Left office/age	Dec 5, 1811/39
Date of death/age	Jun 10, 1824/52
Cabinet service	4y 10m 25d

Rogers, William P.   **AT**

Date of birth	Jun 23, 1913
Date of appointment/age	Jan 27, 1958/44
Assumed office/age	Jan 27, 1958/44
Left office/age	Jan 20, 1961/47
Date of death/age	— — —
Cabinet service	2y 11m 23d

Rogers, William P. **ST**
Date of birth .... Jun 23, 1913
Date of appointment/age .... Dec 12, 1968/55
Assumed office/age .... Jan 21, 1969/55
Left office/age .... Sep 3, 1973/60
Date of death/age .... — — —
Cabinet service 4y 7m 13d

Romney, George W. **HD**
Date of birth .... Jul 8, 1907
Date of appointment/age .... Dec 12, 1968/61
Assumed office/age .... Jan 21, 1969/61
Left office/age .... Nov 28, 1973/66
Date of death/age .... — — —
Cabinet service 4y 10m 7d

Root, Elihu **WR**
Date of birth .... Feb 15, 1845
Date of appointment/age .... Aug 1, 1899/54
Assumed office/age .... Aug 1, 1899/54
Left office/age .... Jan 31, 1904/58
Date of death/age .... Feb 7, 1937/91
Cabinet service 4y 6m

Root, Elihu **ST**
Date of birth .... Feb 15, 1845
Date of appointment/age .... Jul 7, 1905/60
Assumed office/age .... Jul 19, 1905/60
Left office/age .... Jan 26, 1909/63
Date of death/age .... Feb 7, 1937/91
Cabinet service 3y 6m 7d

Roper, Daniel C. **CM**
Date of birth .... Apr 1, 1867
Date of appointment/age .... Mar 4, 1933/65
Assumed office/age .... Mar 4, 1933/65
Left office/age .... Dec 23, 1938/71
Date of death/age .... Apr 11, 1943/76
Cabinet service 5y 9m 19d

Royall, Kenneth C.   **WR**
Date of birth . . . . Jul 24, 1894
Date of appointment/age . . . . Jul 21, 1947/52
Assumed office/age . . . . Jul 25, 1947/53
Left office/age . . . . Sep 17, 1947/53
Date of death/age . . . . May 27, 1971/76
Cabinet service 1m 23d

Rumsfeld, Donald H.   **DF**
Date of birth . . . . Jul 9, 1932
Date of appointment/age . . . . Nov 4, 1975/43
Assumed office/age . . . . Nov 20, 1975/43
Left office/age . . . . Jan 20, 1977/44
Date of death/age . . . . — — —
Cabinet service 1y 2m

Rush, Richard   **AT**
Date of birth . . . . Aug 29, 1780
Date of appointment/age . . . . Feb 10, 1814/33
Assumed office/age . . . . Feb 11, 1814/33
Left office/age . . . . Oct 30, 1817/37
Date of death/age . . . . Jul 30, 1859/78
Cabinet service 3y 8m 19d

Rush, Richard   **TY**
Date of birth . . . . Aug 29, 1780
Date of appointment/age . . . . Mar 7, 1825/44
Assumed office/age . . . . Aug 1, 1825/44
Left office/age . . . . Mar 3, 1829/48
Date of death/age . . . . Jul 30, 1859/78
Cabinet service 3y 7m 2d

Rusk, Dean   **ST**
Date of birth . . . . Feb 9, 1909
Date of appointment/age . . . . Jan 21, 1961/51
Assumed office/age . . . . Jan 21, 1961/51
Left office/age . . . . Jan 20, 1969/59
Date of death/age . . . . — — —
Cabinet service 8y

Rusk, Jeremiah M.   **AG**
Date of birth . . . .   Jun 17, 1830
Date of appointment/age . . . .   Mar 5, 1889/58
Assumed office/age . . . .   Mar 7, 1889/58
Left office/age . . . .   Mar 5, 1893/62
Date of death/age . . . .   Nov 21, 1893/63
Cabinet service 3y 11m 26d

Sargent, John G.   **AT**
Date of birth . . . .   Oct 13, 1860
Date of appointment/age . . . .   Mar 17, 1925/64
Assumed office/age . . . .   Mar 18, 1925/64
Left office/age . . . .   Mar 5, 1929/68
Date of death/age . . . .   Mar 5, 1939/78
Cabinet service 3y 11m 18d

Sawyer, Charles   **CM**
Date of birth . . . .   Feb 10, 1887
Date of appointment/age . . . .   May 6, 1948/61
Assumed office/age . . . .   May 6, 1948/61
Left office/age . . . .   Jan 20, 1953/65
Date of death/age . . . .   Apr 7, 1979/92
Cabinet service 4y 8m 14d

Saxbe, William B.   **AT**
Date of birth . . . .   Jun 24, 1916
Date of appointment/age . . . .   Nov 1, 1973/57
Assumed office/age . . . .   Jan 4, 1974/57
Left office/age . . . .   Dec 14, 1974/58
Date of death/age . . . .   — — —
Cabinet service 11m 10d

Schlesinger, James R.   **DF**
Date of birth . . . .   Feb 15, 1929
Date of appointment/age . . . . —   May 10, 1973/44
Assumed office/age . . . .   Jun 29, 1973/44
Left office/age . . . .   Nov 3, 1975/46
Date of death/age . . . .   — — —
Cabinet service 2y 4m 5d

Schlesinger, James R.   **EN**
Date of birth ....   Feb 15, 1929
Date of appointment/age ....   Aug 5, 1977/48
Assumed office/age ....   Oct 1, 1977/48
Left office/age ....   Aug 25, 1979/50
Date of death/age ....   — — —
Cabinet service 1y 10m 24d

Schofield, John M.   **WR**
Date of birth ....   Sep 29, 1831
Date of appointment/age ....   May 28, 1868/36
Assumed office/age ....   Jun 1, 1868/36
Left office/age ....   Mar 10, 1869/37
Date of death/age ....   Mar 4, 1906/74
Cabinet service 9m 9d

Schurz, Carl   **IN**
Date of birth ....   Mar 2, 1829
Date of appointment/age ....   Mar 12, 1877/48
Assumed office/age ....   Mar 12, 1877/48
Left office/age ....   Mar 7, 1881/52
Date of death/age ....   Mar 14, 1906/77
Cabinet service 3y 11m 23d

Schweiker, Richard S.   **HH**
Date of birth ....   Jun 1, 1926
Date of appointment/age ....   Dec 12, 1980/54
Assumed office/age ....   Jan 22, 1981/54
Left office/age ....   Jan 12, 1983/56
Date of death/age ....   — — —
Cabinet service 1y 11m 21d

Schwellenbach, Lewis B.   **LB**
Date of birth ....   Sep 20, 1894
Date of appointment/age ....   Jun 1, 1945/50
Assumed office/age ....   Jul 1, 1945/50
Left office/age ....   Jun 10, 1948/53
Date of death/age ....   Jun 10, 1948/53
Cabinet service 2y 11m 9d

Seaton, Fred A.   **IN**
Date of birth . . . .   Dec 11, 1909
Date of appointment/age . . . .   Jun 8, 1956/46
Assumed office/age . . . .   Jun 8, 1956/46
Left office/age . . . .   Jan 20, 1961/51
Date of death/age . . . .   Jan 17, 1974/64
Cabinet service 4y 7m 12d

Seward, William H.   **ST**
Date of birth . . . .   May 16, 1801
Date of appointment/age . . . .   Mar 5, 1861/59
Assumed office/age . . . .   Mar 5, 1861/59
Left office/age . . . .   Mar 4, 1869/67
Date of death/age . . . .   Oct 10, 1872/71
Cabinet service 8y

Shaw, Leslie M.   **TY**
Date of birth . . . .   Nov 2, 1848
Date of appointment/age . . . .   Jan 9, 1902/53
Assumed office/age . . . .   Feb 1, 1902/53
Left office/age . . . .   Mar 3, 1907/58
Date of death/age . . . .   Mar 28, 1932/83
Cabinet service 5y 1m 2d

Sherman, John   **TY**
Date of birth . . . .   May 10, 1823
Date of appointment/age . . . .   Mar 8, 1877/53
Assumed office/age . . . .   Mar 10, 1877/53
Left office/age . . . .   Mar 3, 1881/57
Date of death/age . . . .   Oct 22, 1900/77
Cabinet service 3y 11m 23d

Sherman, John   **ST**
Date of birth . . . .   May 10, 1823
Date of appointment/age . . . .   Mar 5, 1897/73
Assumed office/age . . . .   Mar 5, 1897/73
Left office/age . . . .   Apr 27, 1898/74
Date of death/age . . . .   Oct 22, 1900/77
Cabinet service 1y 1m 22d

Sherman, William T.   **WR**
Date of birth .... Feb 8, 1820
Date of appointment/age .... Sep 9, 1869/49
Assumed office/age .... Sep 11, 1869/49
Left office/age .... Oct 31, 1869/49
Date of death/age .... Feb 14, 1891/71
Cabinet service 1m 20d

Shultz, George P.   **LB**
Date of birth .... Dec 13, 1920
Date of appointment/age .... Dec 12, 1968/47
Assumed office/age .... Jan 21, 1969/48
Left office/age .... Jun 18, 1970/49
Date of death/age .... — — —
Cabinet service 1y 4m 28d

Shultz, George P.   **TY**
Date of birth .... Dec 13, 1920
Date of appointment/age .... May 16, 1972/51
Assumed office/age .... Jul 9, 1972/51
Left office/age .... May 1, 1974/53
Date of death/age .... — — —
Cabinet service 1y 10m 22d

Shultz, George P.   **ST**
Date of birth .... Dec 13, 1920
Date of appointment/age .... Jul 26, 1982/61
Assumed office/age .... Jul 15, 1982/61
Left office/age .... — — —
Date of death/age .... — — —
Cabinet service .... — — —

Simon, William E.   **TY**
Date of birth .... Nov 27, 1927
Date of appointment/age .... Apr 18, 1974/46
Assumed office/age .... May 1, 1974/46
Left office/age .... Jan 20, 1977/49
Date of death/age .... — — —
Cabinet service 2y 8m 19d

Smith, Caleb B.   IN
Date of birth ....   Apr 16, 1808
Date of appointment/age ....   Mar 5, 1861/52
Assumed office/age ....   Mar 5, 1861/52
Left office/age ....   Dec 31, 1862/54
Date of death/age ....   Jan 7, 1864/55
Cabinet service 1y 9m 26d

Smith, Charles E.   PG
Date of birth ....   Feb 18, 1842
Date of appointment/age ....   Apr 21, 1898/56
Assumed office/age ....   Apr 21, 1898/56
Left office/age ....   Jan 8, 1902/59
Date of death/age ....   Jan 19, 1908/65
Cabinet service 3y 8m 18d

Smith, Cyrus R.   CM
Date of birth ....   Sep 9, 1899
Date of appointment/age ....   Feb 17, 1968/68
Assumed office/age ....   Mar 2, 1968/68
Left office/age ....   Jan 20, 1969/69
Date of death/age ....   — — —
Cabinet service 10m 18d

Smith, Hoke   IN
Date of birth ....   Sep 2, 1855
Date of appointment/age ....   Mar 6, 1893/37
Assumed office/age ....   Mar 6, 1893/37
Left office/age ....   Aug 31, 1896/40
Date of death/age ....   Nov 27, 1931/76
Cabinet service 3y 5m 25d

Smith, Robert   NV
Date of birth ....   Nov 3, 1757
Date of appointment/age ....   Jul 15, 1801/43
Assumed office/age ....   Jul 27, 1801/43
Left office/age ....   Mar 7, 1809/51
Date of death/age ....   Nov 26, 1842/85
Cabinet service 7y 7m 8d

Smith, Robert   ST
Date of birth .... Nov 3, 1757
Date of appointment/age .... Mar 6, 1809/51
Assumed office/age .... Mar 6, 1809/51
Left office/age .... Apr 6, 1811/53
Date of death/age .... Nov 26, 1842/85
Cabinet service 2y 1m

Smith, William French   AT
Date of birth .... Aug 26, 1917
Date of appointment/age .... Dec 12, 1980/63
Assumed office/age .... Jan 23, 1981/63
Left office/age .... Feb 22, 1985/67
Date of death/age .... — — —
Cabinet service 4y 1m

Snyder, John W.   TY
Date of birth .... Jun 21, 1895
Date of appointment/age .... Jun 12, 1946/50
Assumed office/age .... Jun 25, 1946/51
Left office/age .... Jan 20, 1953/57
Date of death/age .... — — —
Cabinet service 6y 6m 26d

Southard, Samuel L.   NV
Date of birth .... Jun 9, 1787
Date of appointment/age .... Sep 16, 1823/36
Assumed office/age .... Sep 16, 1823/36
Left office/age .... Mar 3, 1829/41
Date of death/age .... Jun 26, 1842/55
Cabinet service 6y 5m 15d

Speed, James   AT
Date of birth .... Mar 11, 1812
Date of appointment/age .... Dec 2, 1864/52
Assumed office/age .... Dec 5, 1864/52
Left office/age .... Jul 16, 1866/54
Date of death/age .... Jun 25, 1887/75
Cabinet service 1y 7m 11d

Spencer, John C.   **WR**
Date of birth ....   Jan 8, 1788
Date of appointment/age ....   Oct 12, 1841/53
Assumed office/age ....   Oct 12, 1841/53
Left office/age ....   Mar 7, 1843/55
Date of death/age ....   May 17, 1855/67
Cabinet service 1y 4m 23d

Spencer, John C.   **TY**
Date of birth ....   Jan 8, 1788
Date of appointment/age ....   Mar 3, 1843/55
Assumed office/age ....   Mar 8, 1843/55
Left office/age ....   May 1, 1844/56
Date of death/age ....   May 17, 1855/67
Cabinet service 1y 1m 24d

Stanbery, Henry   **AT**
Date of birth ....   Feb 20, 1803
Date of appointment/age ....   Jul 23, 1866/63
Assumed office/age ....   Mar 12, 1868/65
Left office/age ....   Jul 20, 1868/65
Date of death/age ....   Jun 26, 1881/78
Cabinet service 4m 8d

Stans, Maurice H.   **CM**
Date of birth ....   Mar 22, 1908
Date of appointment/age ....   Dec 12, 1968/60
Assumed office/age ....   Jan 21, 1969/60
Left office/age ....   Jan 28, 1972/63
Date of death/age ....   — — —
Cabinet service 3y 7d

Stanton, Edwin M.   **AT**
Date of birth ....   Dec 19, 1814
Date of appointment/age ....   Dec 20, 1860/46
Assumed office/age ....   Dec 22, 1860/46
Left office/age ....   Mar 4, 1861/46
Date of death/age ....   Dec 24, 1869/55
Cabinet service 2m 10d

Stanton, Edwin M.   **WR**
Date of birth ....   Dec 19, 1814
Date of appointment/age ....   Jan 15, 1862/47
Assumed office/age ....   Jan 20, 1862/47
Left office/age ....   Aug 12, 1867/52 (suspended)
Date of death/age ....   Dec 24, 1869/55
Cabinet service 5y 6m 23d

Stanton, Edwin M.   **WR**
Date of birth ....   Dec 19, 1814
Date of appointment/age ....   Jan 13, 1868/53 (reinstated)
Assumed office/age ....   Jan 13, 1868/53
Left office/age ....   May 26, 1868/53
Date of death/age ....   Dec 24, 1869/55
Cabinet service 4m 13d

Stettinius, Edward R.   **ST**
Date of birth ....   Oct 22, 1900
Date of appointment/age ....   Nov 30, 1944/44
Assumed office/age ....   Dec 1, 1944/44
Left office/age ....   Jul 2, 1945/44
Date of death/age ....   Oct 31, 1949/49
Cabinet service 7m 1d

Stimson, Henry L.   **WR**
Date of birth ....   Sep 21, 1867
Date of appointment/age ....   May 16, 1911/43
Assumed office/age ....   May 22, 1911/43
Left office/age ....   Mar 4, 1913/45
Date of death/age ....   Oct 20, 1950/83
Cabinet service 1y 9m 10d

Stimson, Henry L.   **ST**
Date of birth ....   Sep 21, 1867
Date of appointment/age ....   Mar 4, 1929/61
Assumed office/age ....   Mar 29, 1929/61
Left office/age ....   Mar 3, 1933/65
Date of death/age ....   Oct 20, 1950/83
Cabinet service 3y 11m 26d

Stimson, Henry L.   **WR**
Date of birth . . . . Sep 21, 1867
Date of appointment/age . . . . Jul 10, 1940/72
Assumed office/age . . . . Jul 10, 1940/72
Left office/age . . . . Sep 26, 1945/78
Date of death/age . . . . Oct 20, 1950/83
Cabinet service 5y 2m 16d

Stoddert, Benjamin   **NV**
Date of birth 1751
Date of appointment/age . . . . May 21, 1798/46
Assumed office/age . . . . Jun 18, 1798/46
Left office/age . . . . Mar 31, 1801/49
Date of death/age . . . . Dec 17, 1813/61
Cabinet service 2y 9m 13d

Stone, Harlan F.   **AT**
Date of birth . . . . Oct 11, 1872
Date of appointment/age . . . . Apr 7, 1924/51
Assumed office/age . . . . Apr 9, 1924/51
Left office/age . . . . Mar 3, 1925/52
Date of death/age . . . . Apr 22, 1946/73
Cabinet service 10m 22d

Straus, Oscar S.   **CL**
Date of birth . . . . Dec 23, 1850
Date of appointment/age . . . . Dec 12, 1906/55
Assumed office/age . . . . Dec 17, 1906/55
Left office/age . . . . Mar 4, 1909/58
Date of death/age . . . . May 3, 1926/75
Cabinet service 2y 2m 13d

Strauss, Lewis L.   **CM**
Date of birth . . . . Jan 31, 1896
Date of appointment/age . . . . Nov 13, 1958/62
Assumed office/age . . . . Nov 13, 1958/62
Left office/age . . . . Aug 9, 1959/63
Date of death/age . . . . Jan 21, 1974/77
Cabinet service 8m 27d

Stuart, Alex H.H.   **IN**
Date of birth .... Apr 2, 1807
Date of appointment/age .... Sep 12, 1850/43
Assumed office/age .... Sep 16, 1850/43
Left office/age .... Mar 6, 1853/45
Date of death/age .... Feb 13, 1891/83
Cabinet service 2y 5m 18d

Summerfield, A.E.   **PG**
Date of birth .... Mar 17, 1899
Date of appointment/age .... Jan 21, 1953/53
Assumed office/age .... Jan 21, 1953/53
Left office/age .... Jan 20, 1961/61
Date of death/age .... Apr 26, 1972/73
Cabinet service 8y

Swanson, Claude A.   **NV**
Date of birth .... Mar 31, 1862
Date of appointment/age .... Mar 4, 1933/70
Assumed office/age .... Mar 4, 1933/70
Left office/age .... Jul 7, 1939/77
Date of death/age .... Jul 7, 1939/77
Cabinet service 6y 4m 3d

Taft, Alphonso   **WR**
Date of birth .... Nov 5, 1810
Date of appointment/age .... Mar 8, 1876/65
Assumed office/age .... Mar 8, 1876/65
Left office/age .... May 31, 1876/65
Date of death/age .... May 21, 1891/80
Cabinet service 2m 23d

Taft, Alphonso   **AT**
Date of birth .... Nov 5, 1810
Date of appointment/age .... May 22, 1876/65
Assumed office/age .... Jun 1, 1876/65
Left office/age .... Mar 11, 1877/66
Date of death/age .... May 21, 1891/80
Cabinet service 9m 10d

Taft, William H.   **WR**
Date of birth . . . . Sep 15, 1857
Date of appointment/age . . . . Jan 11, 1904/46
Assumed office/age . . . . Feb 1, 1904/46
Left office/age . . . . Jun 30, 1908/50
Date of death/age . . . . Mar 8, 1930/72
Cabinet service 4y 4m 29d

Taney, Roger B.   **AT**
Date of birth . . . . Mar 17, 1777
Date of appointment/age . . . . Jul 20, 1831/54
Assumed office/age . . . . Jul 20, 1831/54
Left office/age . . . . Sep 23, 1833/56
Date of death/age . . . . Oct 12, 1864/87
Cabinet service 2y 2m 3d

Taney, Roger B.   **TY**
Date of birth . . . . Mar 17, 1777
Date of appointment/age . . . . Sep 23, 1833/56
Assumed office/age . . . . Sep 23, 1833/56
Left office/age . . . . Jun 24, 1834/57
Date of death/age . . . . Oct 12, 1864/87
Cabinet service 9m 1d

Teller, Henry M.   **IN**
Date of birth . . . . May 23, 1830
Date of appointment/age . . . . Apr 6, 1882/51
Assumed office/age . . . . Apr 17, 1882/51
Left office/age . . . . Mar 3, 1885/54
Date of death/age . . . . Feb 23, 1914/83
Cabinet service 2y 10m 14d

Thomas, Phillip F.   **TY**
Date of birth . . . . Sep 12, 1810
Date of appointment/age . . . . Dec 12, 1860/50
Assumed office/age . . . . Dec 12, 1860/50
Left office/age . . . . Jan 14, 1861/50
Date of death/age . . . . Oct 2, 1890/80
Cabinet service 1m 2d

Thompson, Jacob　　　　　　　　　　**IN**
Date of birth . . . . 　May 15, 1810
Date of appointment/age . . . . 　Mar 6, 1857/46
Assumed office/age . . . . 　Mar 10, 1857/46
Left office/age . . . . 　Jan 9, 1861/50
Date of death/age . . . . 　Mar 24, 1885/74
Cabinet service . . . . 　3y 10m

Thompson, Richard W.　　　　　　　　**NV**
Date of birth . . . . 　Jun 9, 1809
Date of appointment/age . . . . 　Mar 12, 1877/67
Assumed office/age . . . . 　Mar 12, 1877/67
Left office/age . . . . 　Dec 19, 1880/71
Date of death/age . . . . 　Feb 9, 1900/90
Cabinet service . . . . 　3y 9m 7d

Thompson, Smith　　　　　　　　　　**NV**
Date of birth . . . . 　Jan 17, 1768
Date of appointment/age . . . . 　Nov 9, 1818/50
Assumed office/age . . . . 　Jan 1, 1819/50
Left office/age . . . . 　Aug 31, 1823/55
Date of death/age . . . . 　Dec 18, 1843/75
Cabinet service . . . . 　4y 7m

Tobin, Maurice J.　　　　　　　　　　**LB**
Date of birth . . . . 　May 22, 1901
Date of appointment/age . . . . 　Aug 13, 1948/47
Assumed office/age . . . . 　Aug 13, 1948/47
Left office/age . . . . 　Jan 20, 1953/51
Date of death/age . . . . 　Jul 19, 1953/52
Cabinet service . . . . 　4y 5m 7d

Toucey, Isaac　　　　　　　　　　　**AT**
Date of birth . . . . 　Nov 15, 1792
Date of appointment/age . . . . 　Jun 21, 1848/55
Assumed office/age . . . . 　Jun 29, 1848/55
Left office/age . . . . 　Mar 7, 1849/56
Date of death/age . . . . 　Jul 30, 1869/76
Cabinet service . . . . 　8m 7d

Toucey, IsaacNV
Date of birth ....Nov 15, 1792
Date of appointment/age ....Mar 6, 1857/64
Assumed office/age ....Mar 6, 1857/64
Left office/age ....Mar 6, 1861/68
Date of death/age ....Jul 30, 1869/76
Cabinet service 4y

Tracy, Benjamin F.NV
Date of birth ....Apr 26, 1830
Date of appointment/age ....Mar 5, 1889/58
Assumed office/age ....Mar 5, 1889/58
Left office/age ....Mar 5, 1893/62
Date of death/age ....Aug 6, 1915/85
Cabinet service 4y

Trowbridge, Alex B., Jr.CM
Date of birth ....Dec 12, 1929
Date of appointment/age ....May 23, 1967/37
Assumed office/age ....Jun 9, 1967/37
Left office/age ....Feb 29, 1968/38
Date of death/age ....— — —
Cabinet service 8m 20d

Tyner, James N.PG
Date of birth ....Jan 17, 1826
Date of appointment/age ....Jul 12, 1876/50
Assumed office/age ....Jul 12, 1876/50
Left office/age ....Mar 11, 1877/51
Date of death/age ....Dec 6, 1904/78
Cabinet service 7m 29d

Udall, Stewart L.IN
Date of birth ....Jan 31, 1920
Date of appointment/age ....Dec 8, 1960/40
Assumed office/age ....Jan 22, 1961/40
Left office/age ....Jan 20, 1969/48
Date of death/age ....— — —
Cabinet service 7y 11m 28d

Upshur, Abel P.   **NV**
Date of birth ....   Jun 17, 1791
Date of appointment/age ....   Sep 13, 1841/50
Assumed office/age ....   Oct 11, 1841/50
Left office/age ....   Jul 23, 1843/52
Date of death/age ....   Feb 28, 1844/52
Cabinet service 1y 9m 12d

Upshur, Abel P.   **ST**
Date of birth ....   Jun 17, 1791
Date of appointment/age ....   Jul 24, 1843/52
Assumed office/age ....   Jul 24, 1843/52
Left office/age ....   Feb 28, 1844/52
Date of death/age ....   Feb 28, 1844/52
Cabinet service 7m 4d

Usery, Willie J., Jr.   **LB**
Date of birth ....   Dec 21, 1923
Date of appointment/age ....   Jan 23, 1976/52
Assumed office/age ....   Feb 5, 1976/52
Left office/age ....   Jan 20, 1977/53
Date of death/age ....   — — —
Cabinet service 11m 15d

Usher, John P.   **IN**
Date of birth ....   Jan 9, 1816
Date of appointment/age ....   Jan 8, 1863/46
Assumed office/age ....   Jan 8, 1863/46
Left office/age ....   May 14, 1865/49
Date of death/age ....   Apr 13, 1889/73
Cabinet service 2y 4m 6d

Van Buren, Martin   **ST**
Date of birth ....   Dec 5, 1782
Date of appointment/age ....   Mar 6, 1829/46
Assumed office/age ....   Mar 28, 1829/46
Left office/age ....   May 23, 1831/48
Date of death/age ....   Jul 24, 1862/79
Cabinet service 2y 1m 25d

Vance, Cyrus R.   **ST**
Date of birth ....   Mar 27, 1917
Date of appointment/age ....   Dec 4, 1976/59
Assumed office/age ....   Jan 21, 1977/59
Left office/age ....   Apr 30, 1980/63
Date of death/age ....   — — —
Cabinet service 3y 3m 9d

Vilas, William F.   **PG**
Date of birth ....   Jul 9, 1840
Date of appointment/age ....   Mar 6, 1885/44
Assumed office/age ....   Mar 6, 1885/44
Left office/age ....   Jan 15, 1888/47
Date of death/age ....   Aug 27, 1908/68
Cabinet service 2y 10m 9d

Vilas, William F.   **IN**
Date of birth ....   Jul 9, 1840
Date of appointment/age ....   Jan 16, 1888/47
Assumed office/age ....   Jan 16, 1888/47
Left office/age ....   Mar 6, 1889/48
Date of death/age ....   Aug 27, 1908/68
Cabinet service 1y 1m 18d

Vinson, Frederick M.   **TY**
Date of birth ....   Jan 22, 1890
Date of appointment/age ....   Jul 18, 1945/55
Assumed office/age ....   Jul 23, 1945/55
Left office/age ....   Jun 24, 1946/56
Date of death/age ....   Sep 8, 1953/63
Cabinet service 11m 1d

Volpe, John A.   **TR**
Date of birth ....   Dec 8, 1908
Date of appointment/age ....   Dec 12, 1968/60
Assumed office/age ....   Jan 21, 1969/60
Left office/age ....   Jan 20, 1973/64
Date of death/age ....   — — —
Cabinet service 4y

Walker, Frank C.   **PG**
Date of birth .... May 30, 1886
Date of appointment/age .... Sep 10, 1940/54
Assumed office/age .... Sep 10, 1940/54
Left office/age .... May 31, 1945/59
Date of death/age .... Sep 13, 1959/73
Cabinet service 4y 8m 21d

Walker, Robert J.   **TY**
Date of birth .... Jul 19, 1801
Date of appointment/age .... Mar 6, 1845/43
Assumed office/age .... Mar 8, 1845/43
Left office/age .... Mar 5, 1849/47
Date of death/age .... Nov 11, 1869/68
Cabinet service 3y 11m 27d

Wallace, Henry A.   **AG**
Date of birth .... Oct 7, 1888
Date of appointment/age .... Mar 4, 1933/44
Assumed office/age .... Mar 4, 1933/44
Left office/age .... Sep 4, 1940/51
Date of death/age .... Nov 18, 1965/77
Cabinet service 7y 6m

Wallace, Henry A.   **CM**
Date of birth .... Oct 7, 1888
Date of appointment/age .... Mar 1, 1945/56
Assumed office/age .... Mar 2, 1945/56
Left office/age .... Sep 27, 1946/57
Date of death/age .... Nov 18, 1965/77
Cabinet service 1y 7m 25d

Wallace, Henry C.   **AG**
Date of birth .... May 11, 1866
Date of appointment/age .... Mar 5, 1921/54
Assumed office/age .... Mar 5, 1921/54
Left office/age .... Oct 25, 1924/58
Date of death/age .... Oct 25, 1924/58
Cabinet service 3y 7m 20d

Wanamaker, John   **PG**
Date of birth ....   Jul 11, 1838
Date of appointment/age ....   Mar 5, 1889/50
Assumed office/age ....   Mar 5, 1889/50
Left office/age ....   Mar 5, 1893/54
Date of death/age ....   Dec 12, 1922/84
Cabinet service 4y

Washburne, Elihu B.   **ST**
Date of birth ....   Sep 23, 1816
Date of appointment/age ....   Mar 5, 1869/52
Assumed office/age ....   Mar 5, 1869/52
Left office/age ....   Mar 16, 1869/52
Date of death/age ....   Oct 23, 1887/71
Cabinet service 11d

Watson, William Marvin   **PG**
Date of birth ....   Jun 6, 1924
Date of appointment/age ....   Apr 10, 1968/43
Assumed office/age ....   Apr 27, 1968/43
Left office/age ....   Jan 20, 1969/43
Date of death/age ....   — — —
Cabinet service 8m 24d

Watt, James G.   **IN**
Date of birth ....   Jan 31, 1938
Date of appointment/age ....   Dec 23, 1980/42
Assumed office/age ....   Jan 23, 1981/42
Left office/age ....   Nov 19, 1983/45
Date of death/age ....   — — —
Cabinet service 2y 9m 27d

Weaver, Robert C.   **HD**
Date of birth ....   Dec 29, 1907
Date of appointment/age ....   Jan 18, 1966/58
Assumed office/age ....   Jan 18, 1966/58
Left office/age ....   Jan 20, 1969/61
Date of death/age ....   — — —
Cabinet service 3y 2d

Webster, Daniel   **ST**
Date of birth .... Jan 18, 1782
Date of appointment/age .... Mar 5, 1841/59
Assumed office/age .... Mar 5, 1841/59
Left office/age .... May 8, 1843/61
Date of death/age .... Oct 24, 1852/70
Cabinet service 2y 2m 3d

Webster, Daniel   **ST**
Date of birth .... Jan 18, 1782
Date of appointment/age .... Jul 22, 1850/68
Assumed office/age .... Jul 22, 1850/68
Left office/age .... Oct 24, 1852/70
Date of death/age .... Oct 24, 1852/70
Cabinet service 2y 3m 2d

Weeks, John W.   **WR**
Date of birth .... Apr 11, 1860
Date of appointment/age .... Mar 5, 1921/60
Assumed office/age .... Mar 5, 1921/60
Left office/age .... Oct 13, 1925/65
Date of death/age .... Jul 12, 1926/66
Cabinet service 4y 7m 8d

Weeks, Sinclair   **CM**
Date of birth .... Jun 15, 1893
Date of appointment/age .... Jan 21, 1953/59
Assumed office/age .... Jan 21, 1953/59
Left office/age .... Nov 12, 1958/65
Date of death/age .... Jan 27, 1972/78
Cabinet service 4y 9m 22d

Weinberger, Caspar W.   **HW**
Date of birth .... Aug 18, 1917
Date of appointment/age .... Nov 28, 1972/55
Assumed office/age .... Feb 8, 1973/55
Left office/age .... Jun 27, 1975/57
Date of death/age .... — — —
Cabinet service 2y 4m 19d

Weinberger, Caspar W.　　　　　**DF**
Date of birth .... Aug 18, 1917
Date of appointment/age .... Dec 12, 1980/63
Assumed office/age .... Jan 21, 1981/63
Left office/age .... – – –
Date of death/age .... – – –
Cabinet service .... – – –

Welles, Gideon　　　　　　　**NV**
Date of birth .... Jul 1, 1802
Date of appointment/age .... Mar 5, 1861/58
Assumed office/age .... Mar 7, 1861/58
Left office/age .... Mar 3, 1869/66
Date of death/age .... Feb 11, 1878/75
Cabinet service 7y 11m 26d

West, Roy O.　　　　　　　　**IN**
Date of birth .... Oct 27, 1868
Date of appointment/age .... Jan 21, 1929/60
Assumed office/age .... Jan 21, 1929/60
Left office/age .... Mar 4, 1929/60
Date of death/age .... Nov 29, 1958/90
Cabinet service 1m 11d

Whiting, William F.　　　　　**CM**
Date of birth .... Jul 20, 1864
Date of appointment/age .... Dec 11, 1928/64
Assumed office/age .... Dec 11, 1928/64
Left office/age .... Mar 4, 1929/64
Date of death/age .... Aug 31, 1936/72
Cabinet service 2m 21d

Whitney, William C.　　　　　**NV**
Date of birth .... Jul 5, 1841
Date of appointment/age .... Mar 6, 1885/43
Assumed office/age .... Mar 6, 1885/43
Left office/age .... Mar 4, 1889/47
Date of death/age .... Feb 2, 1904/62
Cabinet service 3y 11m 28d

Wickard, Claude R.   **AG**
Date of birth ....   Feb 28, 1893
Date of appointment/age ....   Aug 27, 1940/47
Assumed office/age ....   Sep 5, 1940/47
Left office/age ....   Jun 29, 1945/52
Date of death/age ....   Apr 29, 1967/74
Cabinet service 4y 9m 24d

Wickersham, George W.   **AT**
Date of birth ....   Sep 19, 1858
Date of appointment/age ....   Mar 5, 1909/50
Assumed office/age ....   Mar 5, 1909/50
Left office/age ....   Mar 5, 1913/54
Date of death/age ....   Jan 25, 1936/77
Cabinet service 4y

Wickliffe, Charles A.   **PG**
Date of birth ....   Jun 8, 1788
Date of appointment/age ....   Sep 13, 1841/53
Assumed office/age ....   Oct 13, 1841/53
Left office/age ....   Mar 5, 1845/56
Date of death/age ....   Oct 31, 1869/81
Cabinet service 3y 4m 20d

Wilbur, Curtis, D.   **NV**
Date of birth ....   May 10, 1867
Date of appointment/age ....   Mar 18, 1924/56
Assumed office/age ....   Mar 18, 1924/56
Left office/age ....   Mar 4, 1929/61
Date of death/age ....   Sep 8, 1954/87
Cabinet service 4y 11m 14d

Wilbur, Ray L.   **IN**
Date of birth ....   Apr 13, 1875
Date of appointment/age ....   Mar 5, 1929/53
Assumed office/age ....   Mar 5, 1929/53
Left office/age ....   Mar 3, 1933/57
Date of death/age ....   Jun 26, 1949/74
Cabinet service 3y 11m 28d

Wilkins, William **WR**
Date of birth .... Dec 20, 1779
Date of appointment/age .... Feb 15, 1844/64
Assumed office/age .... Feb 20, 1844/64
Left office/age .... Mar 7, 1845/65
Date of death/age .... Jun 23, 1865/85
Cabinet service 1y 15d

Williams, George H. **AT**
Date of birth .... Mar 26, 1820
Date of appointment/age .... Dec 14, 1871/51
Assumed office/age .... Jan 10, 1872/51
Left office/age .... May 14, 1875/55
Date of death/age .... Apr 4, 1910/90
Cabinet service 3y 4m 4d

Wilson, Charles E. **DF**
Date of birth .... Jul 18, 1890
Date of appointment/age .... Jan 28, 1953/62
Assumed office/age .... Jan 28, 1953/62
Left office/age .... Oct 8, 1957/67
Date of death/age .... Sep 26, 1961/71
Cabinet service 4y 8m 10d

Wilson, James **AG**
Date of birth .... Aug 16, 1836
Date of appointment/age .... Mar 5, 1897/60
Assumed office/age .... Mar 5, 1897/60
Left office/age .... Mar 5, 1913/76
Date of death/age .... Aug 26, 1920/84
Cabinet service 16y

Wilson, William B. **LB**
Date of birth .... Apr 2, 1862
Date of appointment/age .... Mar 5, 1913/50
Assumed office/age .... Mar 5, 1913/50
Left office/age .... Mar 4, 1921/58
Date of death/age .... May 26, 1934/72
Cabinet service 8y

Wilson, William L.   **PG**
Date of birth ....   May 3, 1843
Date of appointment/age ....   Mar 3, 1895/51
Assumed office/age ....   Apr 4, 1895/51
Left office/age ....   Mar 5, 1897/53
Date of death/age ....   Oct 17, 1900/57
Cabinet service 1y 11m 1d

Windom, William   **TY**
Date of birth ....   May 10, 1827
Date of appointment/age ....   Mar 5, 1881/53
Assumed office/age ....   Mar 8, 1881/53
Left office/age ....   Nov 13, 1881/54
Date of death/age ....   Jan 29, 1891/63
Cabinet service 8m 5d

Windom, William   **TY**
Date of birth ....   May 10, 1827
Date of appointment/age ....   Mar 5, 1889/61
Assumed office/age ....   Mar 7, 1889/61
Left office/age ....   Jan 29, 1891/63
Date of death/age ....   Jan 29, 1891/63
Cabinet service 1y 10m 22d

Wirt, William   **AT**
Date of birth ....   Nov 8, 1772
Date of appointment/age ....   Nov 13, 1817/45
Assumed office/age ....   Nov 15, 1817/45
Left office/age ....   Mar 3, 1829/56
Date of death/age ....   Feb 18, 1834/61
Cabinet service 11y 3m 16d

Wirtz, W. Willard   **LB**
Date of birth ....   Mar 14, 1912
Date of appointment/age ....   Sep 25, 1962/50
Assumed office/age ....   Sep 25, 1962/50
Left office/age ....   Jan 20, 1969/56
Date of death/age ....   — — —
Cabinet service 6y 3m 26d

Wolcott, Oliver   **TY**
Date of birth .... Jan 11, 1760
Date of appointment/age .... Feb 2, 1795/35
Assumed office/age .... Feb 2, 1795/35
Left office/age .... Dec 31, 1800/40
Date of death/age .... Jun 1, 1833/73
Cabinet service 5y 10m 29d

Wood, Robert C.   **HD**
Date of birth .... Sep 16, 1923
Date of appointment/age .... Jan 3, 1969/45
Assumed office/age .... Jan 8, 1969/45
Left office/age .... Jan 21, 1969/45
Date of death/age .... — — —
Cabinet service 13d

Woodbury, Levi   **NV**
Date of birth .... Dec 22, 1789
Date of appointment/age .... May 23, 1831/41
Assumed office/age .... May 23, 1831/41
Left office/age .... Jun 29, 1834/44
Date of death/age .... Sep 4, 1851/61
Cabinet service 3y 1m 6d

Woodbury, Levi   **TY**
Date of birth .... Dec 22, 1789
Date of appointment/age .... Jun 27, 1834/44
Assumed office/age .... Jul 1, 1834/44
Left office/age .... Mar 3, 1841/51
Date of death/age .... Sep 4, 1851/61
Cabinet service 6y 8m 2d

Woodin, William H.   **TY**
Date of birth .... May 27, 1868
Date of appointment/age .... Mar 4, 1933/64
Assumed office/age .... Mar 4, 1933/64
Left office/age .... Dec 31, 1933/65
Date of death/age .... May 3, 1934/65
Cabinet service 9m 27d

Woodring, Harry H.   **WR**
Date of birth ....   May 31, 1890
Date of appointment/age ....   May 6, 1937/46
Assumed office/age ....   May 6, 1937/46
Left office/age ....   Jul 9, 1940/50
Date of death/age ....   Sep 9, 1967/77
Cabinet service 3y 2m 3d

Work, Hubert   **PG**
Date of birth ....   Jul 3, 1860
Date of appointment/age ....   Mar 4, 1922/61
Assumed office/age ....   Mar 4, 1922/61
Left office/age ....   Mar 4, 1923/62
Date of death/age ....   Dec 14, 1942/82
Cabinet service 1y

Work, Hubert   **IN**
Date of birth ....   Jul 3, 1860
Date of appointment/age ....   Feb 27, 1923/62
Assumed office/age ....   Mar 5, 1923/62
Left office/age ....   Jul 24, 1928/68
Date of death/age ....   Dec 14, 1942/82
Cabinet service 5y 4m 19d

Wright, Luke E.   **WR**
Date of birth ....   Aug 29, 1846
Date of appointment/age ....   Jun 29, 1908/61
Assumed office/age ....   Jul 1, 1908/61
Left office/age ....   Mar 11, 1909/62
Date of death/age ....   Nov 17, 1922/76
Cabinet service 8m 10d

Wynne, Robert J.   **PG**
Date of birth ....   Nov 18, 1851
Date of appointment/age ....   Oct 10, 1904/52
Assumed office/age ....   Oct 10, 1904/52
Left office/age ....   Mar 5, 1905/53
Date of death/age ....   Mar 11, 1922/70
Cabinet service 4m 23d

Supreme Court Justices

John Jay **CJ** 1789–1795
John Rutledge 1789–1791
William Cushing 1789–1810
James Wilson 1789–1798
John Blair 1789–1796
James Iredell 1790–1799
Thomas Johnson 1791–1793
William Paterson 1793–1806
Samuel Chase 1796–1811
Oliver Ellsworth **CJ** 1796–1800
Bushrod Washington 1798–1829
Alfred Moore 1799–1804
John Marshall 1801–1835
William Johnson 1804–1834
Henry B. Livingston 1806–1823
Thomas Todd 1807–1826
Joseph Story 1811–1845
Gabriel Duval 1811–1835
Smith Thompson 1823–1843
Robert Trimble 1826–1828
John McLean 1829–1861
Henry Baldwin 1830–1844
James M. Wayne 1835–1867
Roger B. Taney **CJ** 1836–1864
Philip P. Barbour 1836–1841
John Catron 1837–1865
John McKinley 1837–1852
Peter V. Daniel 1841–1860
Samuel Nelson 1845–1872
Levi Woodbury 1846–1851
Robert C. Grier 1846–1870
Benjamin R. Curtis 1851–1857
John A. Campbell 1853–1861
Nathan Clifford 1858–1881
Noah H. Swayne 1862–1881

Samuel F. Miller 1862–1890
David Davis 1862–1877
Stephen J. Field 1863–1897
Salmon P. Chase **CJ** 1864–1873
Edwin M. Stanton 1869
William Strong 1870–1880
Joseph P. Bradley 1870–1892
Ward Hunt 1872–1882
Morrison R. Waite **CJ** 1874–1878
John M. Harlan 1877–1911
William B. Woods 1880–1887
Stanley Matthews 1881–1889
Horace Gray 1881–1902
Samuel Blatchford 1882–1893
Lucius Q.C. Lamar 1888–1893
Melville W. Fuller **CJ** 1888–1910
David J. Brewer 1889–1910
Henry B. Brown 1890–1906
George Shiras, Jr. 1892–1903
Howell E. Jackson 1893–1895
Edward D. White **AJ** 1894–1910,
 CJ 1910–1921
Rufus W. Peckham 1895–1909
Joseph McKenna 1898–1925
Oliver W. Holmes 1902–1932
William R. Day 1903–1922
William H. Moody 1906–1910
Horace H. Lurton 1909–1914
Charles E. Hughes **AJ** 1910–1916,
 CJ 1930–1941
Willis Van Devanter 1910–1937
Joseph R. Lamar 1910–1916
Mahlon Pitney 1912–1922
James C. McReynolds 1914–1941
Louis D. Brandeis 1916–1939

John H. Clarke 1916–1922
William H. Taft **CJ** 1921–1930
George Sutherland 1922–1938
Pierce Butler 1922–1939
Edward T. Sanford 1923–1930
Harlan F. Stone **AJ** 1925–1941,
　　CJ 1941–1946
Owen J. Roberts 1930–1945
Benjamin N. Cardozo 1932–1948
Hugo L. Black 1937–1971
Stanley F. Reed 1938–1957
Felix Frankfurter 1939–1962
William O. Douglas 1939–1975
Frank Murphy 1940–1949
James F. Byrnes 1941–1942
Robert H. Jackson 1941–1954
Wiley B. Rutledge 1943–1949
Harold H. Burton 1945–1958

Fred M. Vinson **CJ** 1946–1953
Tom C. Clark 1949–1967
Sherman Minton 1949–1956
Earl Warren **CJ** 1954–1969
John M. Harlan 1955–1971
William J. Brennan, Jr. 1957–
Charles E. Whittaker 1957–1962
Potter Stewart 1959–1981
Byron R. White 1962–
Arthur J. Goldberg 1962–1965
Abe Fortas 1965–1969
Thurgood Marshall 1967–
Warren E. Burger **CJ** 1969–
Harry A. Blackmun 1970–
Lewis F. Powell, Jr. 1971–
William H. Rehnquist 1971–
John Paul Stevens 1975–
Sandra Day O'Connor 1981–

Biographical Data—
Supreme Court Justices

Baldwin, Henry

Date of birth	Jan 14, 1780
Date of appointment/age	Jan 4, 1830/49
Date of confirmation/age	Jan 6, 1830/49
Date of resignation/age.............	— — —
Date of death/age	Apr 21, 1844/64
Years of service/retirement	14y 3m 15d/0

Barbour, Philip P.

Date of birth	May 25, 1783
Date of appointment/age	Dec 28, 1835/52
Date of confirmation/age	Mar 15, 1836/52
Date of resignation/age.............	— — —
Date of death/age	Feb 25, 1841/57
Years of service/retirement	4y 11m 10d/0

Black, Hugo L.

Date of birth	Feb 27, 1886
Date of appointment/age	Aug 12, 1937/51
Date of confirmation/age	Aug 17, 1937/51
Date of resignation/age.............	Sep 18, 1971/85
Date of death/age	Sep 25, 1971/85
Years of service/retirement	34y 1m 1d/7d

Blackmun, Harry A.

Date of birth	Nov 12, 1908
Date of appointment/age	Apr 14, 1970/61
Date of confirmation/age	May 12, 1970/61
Date of resignation/age.............	— — —
Date of death/age	— — —
Years of service/retirement	— — —

Blair, John

Date of birth	1732
Date of appointment/age	Sep 24, 1789/56
Date of confirmation/age	Sep 26, 1789/56
Date of resignation/age.............	Jan 27, 1796/63
Date of death/age	Aug 31, 1800/67
Years of service/retirement	6y 4m 1d/4y 7m 4d

Blatchford, Samuel

Date of birth	Mar 9, 1820
Date of appointment/age	Mar 13, 1882/62
Date of confirmation/age	Mar 27, 1882/62
Date of resignation/age.............	— — —
Date of death/age	Jul 7, 1893/72
Years of service/retirement	11y 3m 10d/0

Bradley, Joseph P.

Date of birth	Mar 14, 1813
Date of appointment/age	Feb 7, 1870/56
Date of confirmation/age	Mar 21, 1870/57
Date of resignation/age.............	— — —
Date of death/age	Jan 22, 1892/78
Years of service/retirement	21y 10m 1d/0

Brandeis, Louis D.

Date of birth	Nov 13, 1856
Date of appointment/age	Jan 28, 1916/59
Date of confirmation/age	Jun 1, 1916/59
Date of resignation/age.............	Feb 13, 1939/82
Date of death/age	Oct 5, 1941/84
Years of service/retirement	22y 8m 12d/2y 7m 22d

Brennan, William J., Jr.

Date of birth	Apr 25, 1906
Date of appointment/age	Oct 16, 1956/50
Date of confirmation/age	Mar 19, 1957/50
Date of resignation/age.............	— — —
Date of death/age	— — —
Years of service/retirement	— — —

Brewer, David J.

Date of birth	Jan 20, 1837
Date of appointment/age	Dec 4, 1889/52
Date of confirmation/age	Dec 18, 1889/52
Date of resignation/age.............	— — —
Date of death/age	Mar 28, 1910/73
Years of service/retirement	20y 3m 10d/0

Brown, Henry B.

Date of birth	Mar 21, 1836
Date of appointment/age	Dec 23, 1890/54
Date of confirmation/age	Dec 29, 1890/54
Date of resignation/age.............	May 28, 1906/70
Date of death/age	Sep 4, 1913/77
Years of service/retirement	15y 4m 29d/7y 3m 7d

Burger, Warren E.

Date of birth	Sep 17, 1907
Date of appointment/age	May 21, 1969/61
Date of confirmation/age	Jun 9, 1969/61
Date of resignation/age.............	— — —
Date of death/age	— — —
Years of service/retirement	— — —

Burton, Harold H.

Date of birth	Jun 22, 1888
Date of appointment/age	Sep 19, 1945/57
Date of confirmation/age	Sep 19, 1945/57
Date of resignation/age.............	Oct 13, 1958/70
Date of death/age	Oct 28, 1964/76
Years of service/retirement	13y 24d/6y 15d

Butler, Pierce

Date of birth	Mar 17, 1866
Date of appointment/age	Nov 23, 1922/56
Date of confirmation/age	Dec 21, 1922/56
Date of resignation/age.............	— — —
Date of death/age	Nov 16, 1939/73
Years of service/retirement	16y 10m 26d/0

Byrnes, James F.

Date of birth	May 2, 1879
Date of appointment/age	Jun 12, 1941/62
Date of confirmation/age	Jun 12, 1941/62
Date of resignation/age............	Oct 3, 1942/63
Date of death/age	Apr 9, 1972/92
Years of service/retirement	1y 3m 21d/29y 6m 6d

Campbell, John A.

Date of birth	Jun 24, 1811
Date of appointment/age	Mar 21, 1853/41
Date of confirmation/age	Mar 25, 1853/41
Date of resignation/age............	Apr , 1861/49
Date of death/age	Mar 12, 1889/77
Years of service/retirement	8y 1m 5d/27y 10m 12d

Cardozo, Benjamin N.

Date of birth	May 24, 1870
Date of appointment/age	Feb 15, 1932/61
Date of confirmation/age	Feb 24, 1932/61
Date of resignation/age............	— — —
Date of death/age	Jul 9, 1938/68
Years of service/retirement	6y 4m 15d/0

Catron, John

Date of birth	1786
Date of appointment/age	Mar 3, 1837/51
Date of confirmation/age	Mar 8, 1837/51
Date of resignation/age............	— — —
Date of death/age	May 30, 1865/79
Years of service/retirement	28y 2m 22d/0

Chase, Salmon P.

Date of birth	Jan 13, 1808
Date of appointment/age	Dec 6, 1864/56
Date of confirmation/age	Dec 6, 1864/56
Date of resignation/age............	— — —
Date of death/age	May 7, 1873/65
Years of service/retirement	8y 5m 1d/0

Chase, Samuel

Date of birth	Apr 17, 1741
Date of appointment/age	Jan 26, 1796/54
Date of confirmation/age	Jan 27, 1796/54
Date of resignation/age.	— — —
Date of death/age	Jun 19, 1811/70
Years of service/retirement	15y 4m 23d/0

Clark, Tom C.

Date of birth	Sep 23, 1899
Date of appointment/age	Aug 2, 1949/49
Date of confirmation/age	Aug 19, 1949/49
Date of resignation/age.	Jun 12, 1967/67
Date of death/age	Jun 13, 1977/77
Years of service/retirement	17y 9m 24d/10y 1d

Clarke, John H.

Date of birth	Sep 18, 1857
Date of appointment/age	Jul 14, 1916/58
Date of confirmation/age	Jul 24, 1916/58
Date of resignation/age.	Sep 18, 1922/65
Date of death/age	Mar 22, 1945/87
Years of service/retirement	6y 1m 24d/22y 6m 4d

Clifford, Nathan

Date of birth	Aug 18, 1803
Date of appointment/age	Dec 9, 1857/54
Date of confirmation/age	Jan 12, 1858/54
Date of resignation/age.	— — —
Date of death/age	Jul 25, 1881/77
Years of service/retirement	23y 6m 13d/0

Curtis, Benjamin R.

Date of birth	Nov 4, 1809
Date of appointment/age	Dec 11, 1851/42
Date of confirmation/age	Dec 29, 1851/42
Date of resignation/age.	Sep 1, 1857/47
Date of death/age	Sep 15, 1874/64
Years of service/retirement	5y 8m 3d/17y 14d

Cushing, William

Date of birth	Mar 1, 1732
Date of appointment/age	Sep 24, 1789/57
Date of confirmation/age	Sep 26, 1789/57
Date of resignation/age.............	— — —
Date of death/age	Sep 13, 1810/78
Years of service/retirement	20y 11m 18d/0

Daniel, Peter V.

Date of birth	Apr 24, 1784
Date of appointment/age	Feb 26, 1841/56
Date of confirmation/age	Mar 2, 1841/56
Date of resignation/age.............	— — —
Date of death/age	May 30, 1860/76
Years of service/retirement	19y 2m 28d/0

Day, William R.

Date of birth	Apr 17, 1849
Date of appointment/age	Feb 19, 1903/53
Date of confirmation/age	Feb 23, 1903/53
Date of resignation/age.............	Nov 13, 1922/73
Date of death/age	Jul 9, 1923/74
Years of service/retirement	19y 8m 21d/7m 26d

Davis, David

Date of birth	Mar 9, 1815
Date of appointment/age	Dec 1, 1862/47
Date of confirmation/age	Dec 8, 1862/47
Date of resignation/age.............	Mar 4, 1877/61
Date of death/age	Jun 26, 1886/70
Years of service/retirement	14y 2m 24d/9y 3m 22d

Douglas, William O.

Date of birth	Oct 16, 1898
Date of appointment/age	Mar 20, 1939/40
Date of confirmation/age	Apr 4, 1939/40
Date of resignation/age.............	Nov 12, 1975/77
Date of death/age	Jan 19, 1980/81
Years of service/retirement	36y 7m 8d/4y 2m 7d

Duval, Gabriel
Date of birth	Dec 6, 1752
Date of appointment/age	Nov 15, 1811/58
Date of confirmation/age	Nov 18, 1811/58
Date of resignation/age.............	Jan , 1835/82
Date of death/age	Mar 6, 1844/91
Years of service/retirement	23y 2m 13d/9y 1m 6d

Ellsworth, Oliver
Date of birth	Apr 29, 1745
Date of appointment/age	Mar 3, 1796/50
Date of confirmation/age	Mar 4, 1796/50
Date of resignation/age.............	Sep 30, 1800/55
Date of death/age	Nov 26, 1807/62
Years of service/retirement	4y 6m 24d/7y 1m 27d

Field, Stephen J.
Date of birth	Nov 4, 1816
Date of appointment/age	Mar 6, 1863/46
Date of confirmation/age	Mar 10, 1863/46
Date of resignation/age.............	Dec 1, 1897/81
Date of death/age	Apr 9, 1899/82
Years of service/retirement	34y 8m 21d/1y 4m 8d

Fortas, Abe
Date of birth	Jun 19, 1910
Date of appointment/age	Jul 28, 1965/55
Date of confirmation/age	Aug 11, 1965/55
Date of resignation/age.............	May 16, 1969/58
Date of death/age	— — —
Years of service/retirement	3y 9m 5d/— — —

Frankfurter, Felix
Date of birth	Nov 15, 1882
Date of appointment/age	Jan 5, 1939/56
Date of confirmation/age	Jan 17, 1939/56
Date of resignation/age.............	Aug 28, 1962/79
Date of death/age	Feb 22, 1965/82
Years of service/retirement	23y 7m 11d/2y 5m 25d

Fuller, Melville W.

Date of birth	Feb 11, 1833
Date of appointment/age	May 2, 1888/54
Date of confirmation/age	Jul 20, 1888/54
Date of resignation/age............	— — —
Date of death/age	Jul 4, 1910/77
Years of service/retirement	21y 11m 14d/0

Goldberg, Arthur J.

Date of birth	Aug 8, 1908
Date of appointment/age	Aug 31, 1962/54
Date of confirmation/age	Sep 25, 1962/54
Date of resignation/age............	Jul 25, 1965/56
Date of death/age	— — —
Years of service/retirement	2y 10m/ — — —

Gray, Horace

Date of birth	Mar 24, 1828
Date of appointment/age	Dec 19, 1881/53
Date of confirmation/age	Dec 20, 1881/53
Date of resignation/age............	Jul 9, 1902/74
Date of death/age	Sep 15, 1902/74
Years of service/retirement	20y 6m 19d/2m 6d

Grier, Robert C.

Date of birth	Mar 5, 1794
Date of appointment/age	Aug 3, 1846/52
Date of confirmation/age	Aug 4, 1846/52
Date of resignation/age............	Jan 31, 1870/75
Date of death/age	Sep 26, 1870/76
Years of service/retirement	23y 5m 27d/7m 26d

Harlan, John M.

Date of birth	Jun 1, 1833
Date of appointment/age	Oct 17, 1877/43
Date of confirmation/age	Nov 29, 1877/43
Date of resignation/age............	— — —
Date of death/age	Oct 14, 1911/77
Years of service/retirement	33y 10m 15d/0

Harlan, John M.
Date of birth	May 20, 1899
Date of appointment/age	Jan 10, 1955/55
Date of confirmation/age	Mar 16, 1955/55
Date of resignation/age.............	— — —
Date of death/age	Dec 29, 1971/72
Years of service/retirement	16y 9m 13d/0

Holmes, Oliver W.
Date of birth	Mar 8, 1841
Date of appointment/age	Dec 2, 1902/61
Date of confirmation/age	Dec 4, 1902/61
Date of resignation/age.............	Jan 12, 1932/90
Date of death/age	Mar 6, 1935/93
Years of service/retirement	29y 1m 8d/3y 1m 20d

Hughes, Charles E.
Date of birth	Apr 11, 1862
Date of appointment/age	Apr 25, 1910/48
Date of confirmation/age	May 2, 1910/48
Date of resignation/age.............	Jun 10, 1916/54
Date of death/age	Aug 27, 1948/86
Years of service/retirement	6y 1m 8d/32y 2m 17d

Hughes, Charles E.
Date of birth	Apr 11, 1862
Date of appointment/age	Feb 3, 1930/67
Date of confirmation/age	Feb 13, 1930/67
Date of resignation/age.............	Jul 1, 1941/79
Date of death/age	Aug 27, 1948/86
Years of service/retirement	11y 4m 18d/7y 1m 26d

Hunt, Ward
Date of birth	Jun 14, 1810
Date of appointment/age	Dec 11, 1872/62
Date of confirmation/age	Dec 11, 1872/62
Date of resignation/age.............	Jan 7, 1882/71
Date of death/age	Mar 24, 1886/75
Years of service/retirement	9y 27d/4y 2m 17d

Iredell, James

Date of birth	Oct 5, 1751
Date of appointment/age	Feb 9, 1790/38
Date of confirmation/age	Feb 10, 1790/38
Date of resignation/age............	— — —
Date of death/age	Oct 2, 1799/47
Years of service/retirement	9y 7m 22d/0

Jackson, Howell E.

Date of birth	Apr 8, 1832
Date of appointment/age	Feb 2, 1893/60
Date of confirmation/age	Feb 18, 1893/60
Date of resignation/age............	— — —
Date of death/age	Aug 8, 1895/63
Years of service/retirement	2y 5m 21d/0

Jackson, Robert H.

Date of birth	Feb 13, 1892
Date of appointment/age	Jun 12, 1941/49
Date of confirmation/age	Jul 7, 1941/49
Date of resignation/age............	— — —
Date of death/age	Oct 9, 1954/62
Years of service/retirement	13y 3m 2d/0

Jay, John

Date of birth	Dec 12, 1745
Date of appointment/age	Sep 24, 1789/43
Date of confirmation/age	Sep 26, 1789/43
Date of resignation/age............	Jun 29, 1791/45
Date of death/age	Jul 23, 1800/54
Years of service/retirement	1y 9m 3d/9y 24d

Johnson, Thomas

Date of birth	Nov 4, 1732
Date of appointment/age	Nov 1, 1791/58
Date of confirmation/age	Nov 7, 1791/59
Date of resignation/age............	Mar 4, 1793/60
Date of death/age	Oct 25, 1819/86
Years of service/retirement	1y 3m 25d/26y 7m 21d

Johnson, William

Date of birth	Dec 27, 1771
Date of appointment/age	Mar 22, 1804/32
Date of confirmation/age	Mar 24, 1804/32
Date of resignation/age.............	— — —
Date of death/age	Aug 4, 1834/62
Years of service/retirement	30y 4m 11d/0

Lamar, Joseph R.

Date of birth	Oct 14, 1857
Date of appointment/age	Dec 12, 1910/52
Date of confirmation/age	Dec 15, 1910/52
Date of resignation/age.............	— — —
Date of death/age	Jan 2, 1916/58
Years of service/retirement	5y 18d/0

Lamar, Lucius Q.C.

Date of birth	Sep 17, 1825
Date of appointment/age	Dec 6, 1887/62
Date of confirmation/age	Jan 16, 1888/62
Date of resignation/age.............	— — —
Date of death/age	Jan 24, 1893/67
Years of service/retirement	5y 8d/0

Livingston, Henry B.

Date of birth	Nov 26, 1757
Date of appointment/age	Dec 13, 1806/49
Date of confirmation/age	Dec 17, 1806/49
Date of resignation/age.............	— — —
Date of death/age	Mar 18, 1823/65
Years of service/retirement	16y 3m 1d/0

Lurton, Horace H.

Date of birth	Feb 26, 1844
Date of appointment/age	Dec 13, 1909/65
Date of confirmation/age	Dec 20, 1909/65
Date of resignation/age.............	— — —
Date of death/age	Jul 12, 1914/70
Years of service/retirement	4y 6m 22d/0

McKenna, Joseph

Date of birth	Aug 10, 1843
Date of appointment/age	Dec 16, 1897/54
Date of confirmation/age	Jan 21, 1898/54
Date of resignation/age	Jan 5, 1925/81
Date of death/age	Nov 21, 1926/83
Years of service/retirement	26y 11m 15d/1y 10m 16d

McKinley, John

Date of birth	May 1, 1780
Date of appointment/age	Sep 18, 1837/57
Date of confirmation/age	Sep 25, 1837/57
Date of resignation/age	— — —
Date of death/age	Jul 19, 1852/72
Years of service/retirement	14y 9m 24d/0

McLean, John

Date of birth	Mar 11, 1785
Date of appointment/age	Feb 16, 1829/43
Date of confirmation/age	Mar 7, 1829/43
Date of resignation/age	— — —
Date of death/age	Apr 4, 1861/76
Years of service/retirement	32y 28d/0

McReynolds, James C.

Date of birth	Feb 3, 1862
Date of appointment/age	Aug 19, 1914/52
Date of confirmation/age	Aug 29, 1914/52
Date of resignation/age	Jan 31, 1941/78
Date of death/age	Aug 24, 1946/84
Years of service/retirement	26y 5m 2d/5y 6m 24d

Marshall, John

Date of birth	Sep 24, 1755
Date of appointment/age	Jan 20, 1801/46
Date of confirmation/age	Jan 27, 1801/46
Date of resignation/age	— — —
Date of death/age	Jul 6, 1835/79
Years of service/retirement	34y 5m 9d/0

Marshall, Thurgood

Date of birth	Jul 2, 1908
Date of appointment/age	Jun 13, 1967/59
Date of confirmation/age	Aug 30, 1967/59
Date of resignation/age	— — —
Date of death/age	— — —
Years of service/retirement	— — —

Matthews, Stanley

Date of birth	Jul 21, 1824
Date of appointment/age	May 21, 1881/56
Date of confirmation/age	May 21, 1881/56
Date of resignation/age	— — —
Date of death/age	Mar 22, 1889/64
Years of service/retirement	7y 10m 1d/0

Miller, Samuel F.

Date of birth	Apr 5, 1816
Date of appointment/age	Jul 16, 1862/46
Date of confirmation/age	Jul 16, 1862/46
Date of resignation/age	— — —
Date of death/age	Oct 14, 1890/74
Years of service/retirement	28y 2m 28d/0

Minton, Sherman

Date of birth	Oct 20, 1890
Date of appointment/age	Sep 15, 1949/58
Date of confirmation/age	Oct 4, 1949/58
Date of resignation/age	Oct 15, 1956/65
Date of death/age	Apr 9, 1965/74
Years of service/retirement	7y 11d/8y 5m 25d

Moody, William H.

Date of birth	Dec 23, 1853
Date of appointment/age	Dec 3, 1906/52
Date of confirmation/age	Dec 12, 1906/52
Date of resignation/age	Nov 20, 1910/56
Date of death/age	Jul 2, 1917/63
Years of service/retirement	3y 11m 8d/6y 7m 12d

Moore, Alfred

Date of birth .... May 21, 1755
Date of appointment/age .... Dec 6, 1799/44
Date of confirmation/age .... Dec 10, 1799/44
Date of resignation/age............ Mar   , 1804/48
Date of death/age .... Oct 15, 1810/55
Years of service/retirement 4y 3m 21d/6y 6m 15d

Murphy, Frank

Date of birth .... Apr 13, 1890
Date of appointment/age .... Jan 4, 1940/49
Date of confirmation/age .... Jan 15, 1940/49
Date of resignation/age............ — — —
Date of death/age .... Jul 19, 1949/59
Years of service/retirement 9y 6m 4d/0

Nelson, Samuel

Date of birth .... Nov 10, 1792
Date of appointment/age .... Feb 14, 1845/52
Date of confirmation/age .... Feb 14, 1845/52
Date of resignation/age............ Nov 28, 1872/80
Date of death/age .... Dec 13, 1873/81
Years of service/retirement 27y 9m 14d/1y 15d

O'Connor, Sandra Day

Date of birth .... Mar 26, 1930
Date of appointment/age .... Jul 7, 1981/51
Date of confirmation/age .... Sep 21, 1981/51
Date of resignation/age............ — — —
Date of death/age .... — — —
Years of service/retirement .... — — —

Paterson, William

Date of birth .... Dec 24, 1745
Date of appointment/age .... Mar 4, 1793/47
Date of confirmation/age .... Mar 4, 1793/47
Date of resignation/age............ — — —
Date of death/age .... Sep 9, 1806/60
Years of service/retirement 13y 6m 5d/0

Peckham, Rufus W.

Date of birth	Nov 8, 1838
Date of appointment/age	Dec 3, 1895/57
Date of confirmation/age	Dec 9, 1895/57
Date of resignation/age.............	— — —
Date of death/age	Oct 24, 1909/70
Years of service/retirement	13y 10m 15d/0

Pitney, Mahlon

Date of birth	Feb 5, 1858
Date of appointment/age	Feb 19, 1912/54
Date of confirmation/age	Mar 13, 1912/54
Date of resignation/age.............	Dec 31, 1922/64
Date of death/age	Dec 9, 1924/66
Years of service/retirement	10y 9m 18d/1y 11m 9d

Powell, Lewis F., Jr.

Date of birth	Sep 19, 1907
Date of appointment/age	Oct 21, 1971/64
Date of confirmation/age	Dec 6, 1971/64
Date of resignation/age.............	— — —
Date of death/age	— — —
Years of service/retirement	— — —

Reed, Stanley F.

Date of birth	Dec 31, 1884
Date of appointment/age	Jan 15, 1938/53
Date of confirmation/age	Jan 25, 1938/53
Date of resignation/age.............	Feb 25, 1957/72
Date of death/age	Apr 3, 1980/95
Years of service/retirement	19y 1m/13y 1m 9d

Rehnquist, William H.

Date of birth	Oct 1, 1924
Date of appointment/age	Oct 21, 1971/47
Date of confirmation/age	Dec 10, 1971/47
Date of resignation/age.............	— — —
Date of death/age	— — —
Years of service/retirement	— — —

Roberts, Owen J.

Date of birth	May 2, 1875
Date of appointment/age	May 9, 1930/55
Date of confirmation/age	May 20, 1930/55
Date of resignation/age.	Jul 31, 1945/70
Date of death/age	May 19, 1955/80
Years of service/retirement	15y 2m 11d/9y 9m 19d

Rutledge, John

Date of birth	Sep , 1739
Date of appointment/age	Sep 24, 1789/49
Date of confirmation/age	Sep 26, 1789/49
Date of resignation/age.	Mar 5, 1791/51
Date of death/age	Jul 18, 1800/60
Years of service/retirement	1y 5m 7d/9y 4m 13d

Rutledge, Wiley B.

Date of birth	Jul 20, 1894
Date of appointment/age	Jan 11, 1943/48
Date of confirmation/age	Feb 8, 1943/48
Date of resignation/age.	— — —
Date of death/age	Sep 9, 1949/55
Years of service/retirement	6y 7m 1d/0

Sanford, Edward T.

Date of birth	Jul 23, 1865
Date of appointment/age	Jan 24, 1923/57
Date of confirmation/age	Jan 29, 1923/57
Date of resignation/age.	— — —
Date of death/age	Mar 8, 1930/64
Years of service/retirement	7y 1m 8d/0

Shiras, George, Jr.

Date of birth	Jan 26, 1832
Date of appointment/age	Jul 19, 1892/60
Date of confirmation/age	Jul 26, 1892/60
Date of resignation/age.	Feb 23, 1903/71
Date of death/age	Aug 21, 1924/92
Years of service/retirement	10y 6m 28d/21y 5m 29d

Stanton, Edwin M.

Date of birth	Dec 19, 1814
Date of appointment/age	Dec 20, 1869/55
Date of confirmation/age	Dec 20, 1869/55
Date of resignation/age.............	— — —
Date of death/age	Dec 24, 1869/55
Years of service/retirement	4d/0

Stevens, John Paul

Date of birth	Apr 20, 1920
Date of appointment/age	Nov 28, 1975/55
Date of confirmation/age	Dec 17, 1975/55
Date of resignation/age.............	— — —
Date of death/age	— — —
Years of service/retirement	— — —

Stewart, Potter

Date of birth	Jan 23, 1915
Date of appointment/age	Jan 17, 1959/43
Date of confirmation/age	May 5, 1959/44
Date of resignation/age.............	Jul 23, 1981/66
Date of death/age	— — —
Years of service/retirement	22y 1m 28d/ — — —

Stone, Harlan F.

Date of birth	Oct 11, 1872
Date of appointment/age	Jan 5, 1925/52
Date of confirmation/age	Feb 5, 1925/52
Date of resignation/age.............	— — —
Date of death/age	Apr 22, 1946/73
Years of service/retirement	21y 2m 17d/0

Story, Joseph

Date of birth	Sep 18, 1779
Date of appointment/age	Nov 15, 1811/32
Date of confirmation/age	Nov 18, 1811/32
Date of resignation/age.............	— — —
Date of death/age	Sep 10, 1845/65
Years of service/retirement	33y 9m 23d/0

Strong, William

Date of birth	Mar 6, 1806
Date of appointment/age	Feb 7, 1870/63
Date of confirmation/age	Feb 18, 1870/63
Date of resignation/age	Dec 14, 1880/74
Date of death/age	Aug 19, 1895/89
Years of service/retirement	10y 9m 26d/14y 8m 5d

Sutherland, George

Date of birth	Mar 25, 1862
Date of appointment/age	Sep 5, 1922/60
Date of confirmation/age	Sep 5, 1922/60
Date of resignation/age	Jan 17, 1938/75
Date of death/age	Jul 18, 1942/80
Years of service/retirement	15y 4m 12d/4y 6m 1d

Swayne, Noah H.

Date of birth	Dec 7, 1804
Date of appointment/age	Jan 21, 1862/57
Date of confirmation/age	Jan 24, 1862/57
Date of resignation/age	Jan 21, 1881/76
Date of death/age	Jun 8, 1884/79
Years of service/retirement	18y 11m 27d/3y 4m 18d

Taft, William H.

Date of birth	Sep 15, 1857
Date of appointment/age	Jun 30, 1921/63
Date of confirmation/age	Jun 30, 1921/63
Date of resignation/age	Feb 3, 1930/72
Date of death/age	Mar 8, 1930/72
Years of service/retirement	8y 7m 4d/1m 5d

Taney, Roger B.

Date of birth	Mar 17, 1777
Date of appointment/age	Dec 28, 1835/58
Date of confirmation/age	Mar 15, 1836/58
Date of resignation/age	— — —
Date of death/age	Oct 12, 1864/87
Years of service/retirement	28y 6m 27d/0

Thompson, Smith

Date of birth	Jan 17, 1768
Date of appointment/age	Sep 1, 1823/55
Date of confirmation/age	Dec 9, 1823/55
Date of resignation/age.............	— — —
Date of death/age	Dec 18, 1843/75
Years of service/retirement	20y 9d/0

Todd, Thomas

Date of birth	Jan 23, 1765
Date of appointment/age	Feb 28, 1807/42
Date of confirmation/age	Mar 3, 1807/42
Date of resignation/age.............	— — —
Date of death/age	Feb 7, 1826/61
Years of service/retirement	18y 11m 4d/0

Trimble, Robert

Date of birth	1777
Date of appointment/age	Apr 11, 1826/49
Date of confirmation/age	May 9, 1826/49
Date of resignation/age.............	— — —
Date of death/age	Aug 25, 1828/51
Years of service/retirement	2y 3m 16d/0

Van Devanter, Willis

Date of birth	Apr 17, 1859
Date of appointment/age	Dec 12, 1910/51
Date of confirmation/age	Dec 15, 1910/51
Date of resignation/age.............	Jun 2, 1937/78
Date of death/age	Feb 8, 1951/91
Years of service/retirement	26y 5m 18d/13y 8m 6d

Vinson, Fred M.

Date of birth	Jan 22, 1890
Date of appointment/age	Jun 6, 1946/56
Date of confirmation/age	Jun 20, 1946/56
Date of resignation/age.............	— — —
Date of death/age	Sep 8, 1953/63
Years of service/retirement	7y 2m 19d/0

Waite, Morrison R.
Date of birth	Nov 29, 1816
Date of appointment/age	Jan 19, 1874/57
Date of confirmation/age	Jan 21, 1874/57
Date of resignation/age............	— — —
Date of death/age	Mar 23, 1888/71
Years of service/retirement	14y 2m 2d/0

Warren, Earl
Date of birth	Mar 19, 1891
Date of appointment/age	Sep 30, 1953/62
Date of confirmation/age	Mar 1, 1954/62
Date of resignation/age............	Jun 24, 1969/78
Date of death/age	Jul 9, 1974/83
Years of service/retirement	15y 3m 23d/5y 15d

Washington, Bushrod
Date of birth	Jun 5, 1762
Date of appointment/age	Sep 29, 1798/36
Date of confirmation/age	Dec 20, 1798/36
Date of resignation/age............	— — —
Date of death/age	Nov 26, 1829/67
Years of service/retirement	30y 11m 6d/0

Wayne, James M.
Date of birth	1790
Date of appointment/age	Jan 7, 1835/45
Date of confirmation/age	Jan 9, 1835/45
Date of resignation/age............	— — —
Date of death/age	Jul 5, 1867/77
Years of service/retirement	32y 5m 26d/0

White, Byron R.
Date of birth	Jun 8, 1917
Date of appointment/age	Apr 3, 1962/44
Date of confirmation/age	Apr 11, 1962/44
Date of resignation/age............	— — —
Date of death/age	— — —
Years of service/retirement	— — —

White, Edward D.

Date of birth	Nov 3, 1845
Date of appointment/age	Feb 19, 1894/48
Date of confirmation/age	Feb 19, 1894/48
Date of resignation/age.	— — —
Date of death/age	May 19, 1921/75
Years of service/retirement	27y 3m/0

Whittaker, Charles E.

Date of birth	Feb 22, 1901
Date of appointment/age	Mar 2, 1957/56
Date of confirmation/age	Mar 19, 1957/56
Date of resignation/age.	Apr 1, 1962/61
Date of death/age	Nov 26, 1973/72
Years of service/retirement	5y 13d/11y 7m 25d

Wilson, James

Date of birth	Sep 14, 1742
Date of appointment/age	Sep 24, 1789/47
Date of confirmation/age	Sep 26, 1789/47
Date of resignation/age.	— — —
Date of death/age	Aug 21, 1798/55
Years of service/retirement	8y 10m 26d/0

Woodbury, Levi

Date of birth	Dec 22, 1789
Date of appointment/age	Dec 23, 1845/56
Date of confirmation/age	Jan 3, 1846/56
Date of resignation/age.	— — —
Date of death/age	Sep 4, 1851/61
Years of service/retirement	5y 8m 1d/0

Woods, William B.

Date of birth	Aug 3, 1824
Date of appointment/age	Dec 15, 1880/56
Date of confirmation/age	Dec 21, 1880/56
Date of resignation/age.	— — —
Date of death/age	May 14, 1887/62
Years of service/retirement	6y 4m 23d/0

Index